For Olga —

With thanks for a long

friendship.

John Cerorski

May 1985

Fragmenta Regalia

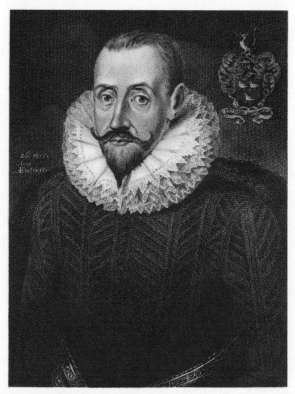

SIR ROBERT NAUNTON.
*Courtesy of the Newberry Library,
Chicago.*

Fragmenta Regalia

or

Observations on Queen Elizabeth,
Her Times & Favorites

Sir Robert Naunton

Edited by
John S. Cerovski

Folger Books
Washington: The Folger Shakespeare Library
London and Toronto: Associated University Presses

© 1985 by Associated University Presses, Inc.

Associated University Presses
440 Forsgate Drive
Cranbury, N.J. 08512

Associated University Presses
25 Sicilian Avenue
London WC1A 2QH, England

Associated University Presses
2133 Royal Windsor Drive
Unit 1
Mississauga, Ontario
Canada L5J 1K5

The frontispiece portrait, from James Caulfield's *Memoirs of Sir Robert Naunton, Knt.*, is used through the courtesy of the Newberry Library, Chicago, Illinois.

The other portraits, engravings by Robert Cooper, are from the 1824 edition of *Fragmenta Regalia*, published by James Baldwyn.

Library of Congress Cataloging in Publication Data

Naunton, Robert, Sir, 1563–1635.
  Fragmenta regalia, or Observations on Queen Elizabeth.

  Bibliography: p.
  Includes index.
  1. Great Britain—Court and courtiers—Biography.
  2. Elizabeth I, Queen of England, 1533–1603.
  3. Great Britain—History—Elizabeth, 1558–1603.
  4. Naunton, Robert, Sir, 1563–1635. I. Cerovski,
John S., 1922–   . II. Title. III. Title: Observations on Queen Elizabeth.
DA358.A1N38   1984   942.05′5   82-49310
ISBN 0-918016-71-1

Printed in the United States of America

To Ann Rose Yates

Contents

Foreword

Sir Robert Naunton's *Fragmenta Regalia* has always been a popular work. After its first appearance in print in 1641, it went through five editions within twelve years, no mean record in the seventeenth century. Since that time it has seldom been out of print. The work's initial popularity was undoubtedly due to the fact that it was one of the few available histories of the Elizabethan reign. Later readers have always found the work attractive for the note of intimacy with suggestions of scandal with which much of the work is infused.

The *Fragmenta* has always been important to historians and biographers as a source of information. Although Naunton was sometimes incorrect, obscure, and often not even original, for some observations—of events and personalities—he is the only source, and for others he is an important corroborator.

Considering the work's popularity and importance, one is surprised to find that there has not been a carefully prepared edition of its text. The first editions, all posthumous, were based on corrupt copies of Naunton's work, and the succeeding editions have been only a degree better. Except for one unsuccessful attempt— the 1824 edition—there has been no search made beyond the printed editions to establish a sound textual basis for the work. For the present edition such a search was made, and I believe that the manuscript copy of Naunton's work used offers not only a more complete text but also a more authentic one than any found in the previous editions.

In keeping with the other texts in the Folger Documents of Tudor and Stuart Civilization, the spelling, punctuation, and capitalization of the text, and also of quotations from contemporary documents, have been modernized.

I wish to thank Dr. Louis B. Wright and the staff of the Folger

Shakespeare Library for their assistance while I worked there. I made frequent use of the Northwestern University Library in Evanston, Illinois, and the Newberry Library in Chicago, and I always found the staff members in both places very helpful.

My greatest indebtedness, however, is to Professor Virgil B. Heltzel, who guided my work in its dissertation form at Northwestern University with patience and generosity in sharing the splendid abundance of his knowledge of Elizabethan England.

JOHN S. CEROVSKI

Fragmenta Regalia

1
The Life of Sir Robert Naunton

Robert Naunton, the eldest son of Henry Naunton of Alderton, Suffolk, and of Elizabeth Ashby, was born in Alderton in 1563.[1] He was the grandson of William Naunton, whose wife, Elizabeth, was the daughter of Sir Anthony Wingfield, K.G. Robert was educated at Cambridge, where he matriculated as a pensioner of Trinity College at Lent 1579,[2] was elected a scholar on 11 November 1582, and graduated B.A. the same year. On 2 October 1585, he became a minor fellow, on 15 March 1586 a major fellow, and received his M.A. soon afterward. In 1587 Naunton was a contributor to the memorial volume, *Academiae Cantabrigiensis Lachrymae,* a collection of poems written in honor of Sir Philip Sidney.[3]

In 1589 Naunton entered the service of his uncle, William Ashby, who was the English ambassador to Scotland. Ashby, in August of 1588, had incurred the displeasure of the court by exceeding the terms of his commission in negotiations with King James for the continued neutrality of Scotland during the Spanish crisis. However, by the end of September an agreement had been reached with terms satisfactory to the court.[4] During Naunton's service in 1589 Ashby was seeking his own revocation from the embassy because of ill health and the lack of financial support for his maintenance there.[5] Naunton's position was that of secretary and courier. It was apparently in this year that he had his first contact with the court figures about whom he was later to write. On 9 July he was in London to solicit Walsingham and Burghley for Ashby's revocation. The following week he had interviews with both men, who told him that they had presented Ashby's suit to the Queen, "but as yet she was neither off nor on but remained uncertain, upon the uncertainty of the state there."⁶ A decision was not reached until December on who would be Ashby's successor, and it was not until the end of January in the following year that Ashby was able to leave Scotland. At that time he wrote to Henry Naunton to commend Robert's service and behavior, and reassured him that "the spending of his time abroad has been in no way prejudicial to his progress in study."⁷

After Ashby's retirement, Naunton went to London.⁸ During the preceding year he had not found court affairs much to his liking,⁹ and it is probable that he did not now find employment there. He was deprived of his uncle's sponsorship by the latter's continued ill health and his death in December 1593.¹⁰ By that time, however, Naunton had returned to Cambridge and in 1592 was elected a fellow of Trinity Hall. His uncle had been instrumental in securing this position for him through the influence of Secretary Walsingham in letters written before the Secretary's death.¹¹ In 1594 Naunton was made public orator of the university.

In 1596 Naunton received permission from the crown to travel on the Continent for three years.¹² The permit was probably obtained through the Earl of Essex, for whose service Naunton's study of politics and languages abroad was to be a preparation. Possibly Naunton's position was of an official nature since he is referred to later as having traveled on "Her Majesty's service."¹³ If so, it was probably merely as a courier bearing letters from the court with him when he left for France in January 1596.¹⁴ He also carried a letter from Essex to the fugitive Spanish Secretary of State, Antonio Pérez, in which Essex called Naunton his friend and asked Pérez to grant him his "love and protection."¹⁵

Essex had established a relationship with Pérez during the latter's visit to England in 1593 and considered him a valuable source of information, not only in regard to the affairs of Spain but also the intrigues of the French court.¹⁶ Naunton remained with Pérez for the next three months and wrote frequently to Essex about the Spaniard's activities and opinions as well as what news and gossip he could obtain about the French political situation. Naunton's letters are in the form of reports, and his position was obviously that of a member of Essex's extensive intelligence service. On 3 March 1596 he wrote:

I shall think mine own staying about him [Pérez] and endeavors most happily employed if they may yield the least contentment or use to your honor by these frank advertisings what I find. But for entering into any course of persuading him either this way or that, I have not presumed so far, having no order from your lordship but to second his humor as best I could. I am now advised . . . to crave some piece of farther instruction from your lordship how I may employ any such small interest as in continuance of time I may gain in him by such daily offices as pass between us to bend or incline him this way or that.[17]

Naunton returned to England at the end of April, which was about the same time Pérez arrived in the company of the Duke de Bouillon, who was to begin negotiations for an Anglo-French alliance.[18] Essex expressed his regard for Naunton's services in a letter dated 20 May 1596:

Mr. Naunton,
    I thank you for your letter, but my thanks must be short. That which concerneth Antonio Pérez, I have answered in a letter to himself. For you I say that though I have care of him, I would have no inconvenience befall you. If you can in some convenient time dispatch your business, I will either send for you if you do like to be a seaman and direct you how you shall come well to me; or give you a task in any place where you would most willingly be, for I would not have you rust.

                                    Your most assured friend,
                                    Essex[19]

In September Naunton attended the Duke de Bouillon to Holland. He was accompanied by Mr. Vernon, a young gentleman committed to his care by Essex. Two months later he went on to Rouen, where he reestablished his contact with Antonio Pérez.[20] During this time he continued to write letters of intelligence to Essex. Although conscientiously fulfilling his obligations to his employer, Naunton became increasingly dissatisfied with the nature of his position. In a letter to Essex, dated 29 November 1596, he wrote:

My sole contentment with myself is my constancy of devotion to your lordship. For other contentments in this course I find them so small as I would loath your lordship should be thought too much beholden for my cause, especially where I find so small means or likelihood of bettering or enabling myself to do your lordship service. It were to small purpose now to allege what I have abidden, and how much more than ever I durst have promised of myself in all kinds of patience both in mind and body. It shall be sufficient if I may, without accusing any other, excuse mine own weakness that can endure this life no longer. The best allowance of credit I can have here is but in nature of betwixt a pedagogue [because of having Mr. Vernon under his care] and a spy, both trades I know not whether more odious or base, as well in their eyes with whom I live as in mine own.[21]

In spite of his discontent Naunton remained with Pérez and accompanied him to Paris in March of 1597.[22] Essex tried to assuage his ill feelings:

If my leisure were as great as is my affection to you, I would send you as many answers as I received letters from you. But I am in a place where I am tied to infinite attendance, and am tied to entertain many businesses and have a fortune of great exercise. And therefore, I am sure you will not look for many compliments from me; and for directions, you need them not. . . . The Queen is every day more and more pleased with your letters and doth promise me she will not let your skill rest. I do truly protest that I read no man's writing with more contentment, nor ever saw any man so much and so fast by any such like improve himself. Therefore let the pains you have taken and incommodities you daily suffer, not discourage you.[23]

During the following summer Naunton once more attempted to break away from his employment and particularly his station with Pérez, but upon direct orders from Essex, who was about to start on the Azores expedition, he was forbidden to do so. In November he complained that he had only one of the three years of his permit left and still had not accomplished his original purpose to travel and study. It was not until the following February (in 1598) that he was able to leave Paris and Pérez and go on to Orléans.[24] One year later, March 1599, Naunton returned to England and his position at Cambridge.[25]

Besides performing his duties as orator at Cambridge, Naunton spent the next few years in trying to recover a sum of money from his uncle's estate, which he had left in trust with Robert Chester and Henry Tuckfield, both Cambridge men,[26] before he went overseas, and which they had misappropriated.[27] A settlement was not reached in the case until July 1602, when the Lord Keeper, Sir Thomas Egerton, issued a decree in Naunton's favor.[28]

In 1601 Naunton was made a proctor at Cambridge while he continued in the position of university orator. At this time Naunton received favorable recognition from Secretary Robert Cecil, who used his influence to advance him in the following years.[29] He was also received with favor by King James, after the latter's accession to the English throne in 1603, at a speech Naunton made on behalf of Cambridge at Hinchinbrook. It is possible that this was a renewal of a contact made initially during Naunton's stay in Scotland in 1589. In a letter to Sir John Coke in April 1604, Naunton described his first visit to the King's presence chamber.[30] According to James Howell, it was about this time that Naunton accompanied the Earl of Rutland on an embassy to Denmark and broke down while making a formal address at the Danish court.[31]

Naunton entered Parliament as a member for Helston, Cornwall, in May 1606. During the following years he divided his time between Cambridge and London. In 1612 he was instrumental in obtaining a position for the barrister James Whitelocke as counsel at Windsor.[32] In April 1614 he was rumored to be one of the most likely candidates to succeed Sir Ralph Winwood as ambassador at The Hague.[33] He was knighted at Windsor on 7 September 1615.[34]

About this time Naunton secured the influence of the King's favorite, George Villiers, the Duke of Buckingham, to whom he was related, and his preferment to court appointments followed rapidly.[35] In June 1616 Naunton was sworn in as Master of Requests. In the following winter he was made Surveyor of the Court of Wards, "a place," according to Whitelocke, "ever held by men learned in law . . . and this man a scholar, but mere stranger to the law." John Chamberlain wrote that "it is marveled that in his declining age, when neither his eyes nor his ears *satis officium suum faciunt*, he should be so ambitious to come upon the stage and show his defects."[36] Naunton was then fifty-three years old.

In October 1617 Sir Ralph Winwood, the Secretary of State, died, and Naunton was spoken of as his possible successor, "being

Sir Robert Naunton

Buckingham's creature."[37] Naunton received the appointment and was sworn in on 8 January 1618. It was said that in return for this appointment he turned over to Buckingham offices held from the crown to the value of 1,000 pounds yearly and promised to make the favorite's younger brother, Christopher Villiers, heir to 500 pounds a year from his hereditary possessions. When he made the appointment the King said that he had "destinated him to it presently upon the decease of Sir Rafe Winwood, though he acquainted no body with it till now, further that he did it *motu proprio*, and *ex certa scientia* of his sufficiency, without any other mediation, and gave him many good lessons, but specially of agreeing and drawing in one line with his fellow Secretary."[38] Naunton's "fellow Secretary" was Sir Thomas Lake. In a letter to John Coke on 11 January, Naunton wrote, "It hath pleased God to incline the King's Majesty to call me their unworthy servant to the place."[39] It was at this time that James adopted the practice of employing two principal secretaries. With the increasing influence of Buckingham the position of the secretaries was relegated to handling routine although important business and presented no opportunity to make decisions regarding state policy.[40] After the dismissal of Lake in February 1618, Sir George Calvert was appointed to his place because, said popular talk, the King "would not have a more eminent man, for fear of reflecting on Sec. Naunton."[41] According to a contemporary historian, the choice was made to balance Naunton's strong Protestant leanings, "Calvert being an Hispaniolized papist: the King matching them together, like contrary elements, to find a medium betwixt them."[42] The subservient position to which the secretaryship had fallen is attested to in a letter written by Chamberlain the following May:

> I hear no news nor speech of Secretary Naunton, no more in a manner than if there were no such man in *rerum natura*, which is a strange kind of obscurity for a man of his place to lie so close and hidden that he should scant be seen or heard of at home.[43]

However, Naunton's conscientious fulfillment of his duties was recognized by Francis Bacon in a report to Buckingham in which he comments that "Secretary Naunton forgets nothing."[44]

Naunton emerged from obscurity in the following months to

play an unfavorable role in the imprisonment and .execution of Sir Walter Ralegh. On 10 August Naunton endorsed the inventory of belongings taken from Ralegh's person after his attempted escape to France the previous night and his return to the Tower for his final imprisonment.[45] Naunton was a principal figure in the crown's plot to obtain sufficient admissions of guilt from Ralegh for his condemnation. For this purpose he hired the services of Sir Thomas Wilson, who had been a spy for Robert Cecil.[46] On 14 September Naunton directed the Lieutenant of the Tower to place Ralegh, with Wilson, in closer confinement, to replace Ralegh's servant with one of Wilson's, and to permit the surgeons to see Ralegh only in the presence of Wilson or his servant. The following week Naunton reprimanded Wilson for exceeding his orders by promising Ralegh "His Majesty's mercy" as a bait to obtain a confession when he should only have held out "hopes" to him, as was usual in examining prisoners. Wilson answered that he never gave Ralegh any hopes of mercy as coming from the King but only as from himself. Naunton also intercepted and examined the letters written by Ralegh and his wife.[47] He was a member of the commission appointed by the King for the examination of Ralegh.[48] On 20 October the King rejected the commission's proposals for issuing a printed statement of the charges against Ralegh as being insufficient, and for a public appearance before the Privy Council because it would make him too popular. Instead, the King proposed that Ralegh should be called before the commission again to be charged and sentenced.[49] This was the course followed. The commission validated the 1603 treason charge against Ralegh and ordered his execution.[50]

Ralegh was executed on 29 October 1618. Three weeks later, Chamberlain, in a letter to Dudley Carlton, the ambassador to The Hague, wrote:

> We are so full still of Sir Walter Ralegh that almost every day brings forth . . . diverse ballads whereof some are called in, and the rest such poor stuff as are not worth the overlooking. But when this heat is somewhat allayed, we shall have a declaration touching him, that shall contradict much of that he protested with so great asseveration, but the proofs had need be very pregnant and demonstrative, or else they will hardly prevail.

The other verses go abroad in the King's and S.N. [Secretary Naunton's] name, though I never heard before that he had the virtue of versifying, and I should have thought he had not now the leisure.[51]

The "declaration" defending the crown's action against Ralegh was published on 27 November[52] and was thought to be the work of Naunton, Bacon, and Yelverton, the Attorney General.[53] Popular report credited Naunton with a considerable share of the responsibility for Ralegh's execution. Thomas Fuller relates the following "pleasant passage":

One Mr. Wiemark, a wealthy man, great novelant [i.e., a newsmonger], and constant Paul's-walker [one who frequents St. Paul's as a lounger or gossip—*OED*], hearing the news that day of the beheading of Sir Walter Ralegh, "His head," said he, "would do very well on the shoulders of Sir Robert Naunton, secretary of state." These words were complained of, and Wiemark summoned to the Privy Council, where he pleaded for himself, that he intended no disrespect to Mr. Secretary, whose known worth was above all detraction; only he spoke in reference to an old proverb, "Two heads are better than one." And so for the present he was dismissed. Not long after, when rich men were called on for a contribution to St. Paul's, Wiemark at the council table subscribed a hundred pounds: but Mr. Secretary told him two hundred were better than one; which, betwixt fear and charity, Wiemark was fain to subscribe.[54]

Although during the next two years Naunton handled mostly routine matters of state, yet it was the office of the Secretary that was responsible for much of the everyday administration and government of the country.[55] Much of his time was taken with correspondence and negotiations regarding the assistance to be granted to the King's son-in-law, the Elector Frederick in Bohemia.[56] Naunton, a strong Protestant, worked at soliciting money to send to the Elector.[57] At this time he was said to have had more frequent access to the King than any other minister,[58] and was referred to as "Honest Naunton."[59] However, his "slow and sour austerity" was also noted, and it was rumored that he was to be made Lord High Treasurer because "so earnest are they to remove him whether

higher or lower."[60] In a letter dated 8 May 1620, Naunton complained to Buckingham of ill health as a result of his "true zeal to
His Majesty's service" and that he had not had a free day in two
years.[61] In September 1619, Naunton had married Penelope, the
daughter of Sir Thomas Perrot, and changed his residence from the
court to a house by Charing Cross. One year later, in September
1620, a daughter was born.[62]

Naunton, probably because of his Protestantism, had gained the
enmity of the Count of Gondomar, the Spanish ambassador to
England. In September 1620 the first of a series of incidents occurred that eventually resulted in the Secretary's dismissal. Gondomar, while calling on Naunton to secure his interest for "certain
individuals," began "out of all reason, to make complaint against
him, breaking out angrily into threats and loud words . . . desiring
in short to obtain by rigor and sharpness what he could not get by
milder methods."[63] Naunton behaved with great calmness but reported the incident to the King. News of the encounter spread
rapidly. Popular opinion sided with Naunton and against Gondomar, who had "carried himself so arrogantly and insolently as if
all our counselors were petty companions in respect of him the
great ambassador (as he calls himself) of the great King of Spain."[64]
A few weeks later Gondomar complained strongly to the King that
Naunton had treated him badly and that he was a bitter persecutor
of the Catholics. The King replied "with some sharpness" that his
ministers must be respected and said that it was not customary for
his secretaries to do anything of importance without his approval.[65]

On 10 January 1621, besides his duties as Secretary and Privy
Councillor, Naunton entered Parliament as a member for Cambridge University.[66] His attendance there, however, lasted only a
few days when he fell out of favor with the King, was suspended
from the secretaryship, and confined to his home.[67] No official
statement was made of the reason for Naunton's suspension, but
the most widely circulated report was that it was due to an overreaching of his authority. It appears, however, to have been merely
an indiscretion of speech. At that time the French ambassador
Cadenet was in London to attempt negotiations for a marriage
between Prince Charles and Princess Henrietta Maria. Naunton,
in a talk with La Forêt, a member of the ambassador's party, said,
on his own responsibility, that when such negotiations were pro-

moted on previous occasions it clearly appeared that they were simply desired to break up similar negotiations with Spain, but as the English were short of money France would undoubtedly have to offer as large a dowry as Spain.[68] A second report was that Naunton had been carrying on a secret correspondence with Baron Dona, the Bohemian ambassador.[69] Almost all the reports credited the Spaniard Gondomar with instigating the action against Naunton, and a few months later the King himself was reported as saying that it was at the request of the Spanish that he ordered the Secretary's suspension.[70]

Naunton was released from confinement in August.[71] Although the King did not restore him to favor, the Secretary continued to keep the seals of his office and to perform some official duties during the succeeding year.[72] In a letter to Buckingham in September 1622, Naunton begged to be retained in office until his wife's current pregnancy was over, since he was "grown in years, and cannot expect many children," and that it was beyond his expectation that she had conceived again after a miscarriage brought on by his troubles during the preceding year.[73] Naunton's request was granted, and his wife gave birth to a son in December.[74] The seals of the secretaryship were taken from him on 16 January 1623, and Sir Edward Conway was sworn in as his successor.[75] Naunton was granted a pension of 1,000 pounds a year, and retained his position on the Privy Council.

In April Naunton applied for the vacant provostship of Eton but was refused. In May he was once more confined to his house on orders from the King and suspended from appearing in the Privy Council, probably as a result of being too outspoken in criticism of the voyage of Buckingham and Prince Charles to Spain to close the negotiations for Charles's marriage to the Infanta.[76] In the following October, still in confinement, he wrote to Buckingham to congratulate him on his safe return.

In January 1624 Naunton once more received the appointment to Parliament from Cambridge.[77] In a letter to Buckingham he wrote that since it was at the King's wish that he received the appointment, he hoped not to appear there "a less person than before," and that he relied on the King's promises to give him a position "equal to or better" than the one he had held.[78] In July it was rumored that he was being considered for the place of Master of the Court of Wards, and public opinion was that "it were pity such places should be given *au plus offrant et dernier encheris-seur.*"[79] Naunton received the King's promise of the position and on 16 July wrote a letter of thanks. In August, through the intercession of Buckingham, he finally received a full release from the confinement imposed on him in the preceding year.[80] On 30 September 1624, the office of Master of the Court of Wards was granted to Naunton for life.[81]

On 12 March 1625, Naunton's son, James, died at the age of two years.[82] On 27 March King James died, and Naunton, as a member of the Privy Council, signed the proclamation of his death and of the accession of Charles.[83] In the following month he was reappointed by Cambridge to sit in Charles's first parliament, and in the following year he was a member for Suffolk.[84]

In the final ten years of his life Naunton continued as Master of the Court of Wards and Privy Councillor but complained more and more of ill health.[85] In July 1634 he made a trip to Tunbridge Wells in a vain effort to improve his condition.[86] By then he was bedridden because of a paralysis of his lower extremities.[87] In August he was taken to his family home at Letheringham, Suffolk.[88] In February 1635 an effort was made to get Naunton to resign as Master of the Court of Wards, but he refused to do so. It was not until the King appointed a commission to decide on his ability to continue in office that he finally surrendered his patent and seals on 17 March. Naunton died ten days later, on Good Friday, 27 March 1635.[89]

2

Naunton's Work

The Date of Composition

The *Fragmenta Regalia* was not published until six years after Naunton's death, and the early editions give no indication of the date of its composition. In spite of the work's great popularity, there appears to be no contemporary reference to it. Dating the work, therefore, is dependent upon the examination of internal evidence.

The work was certainly written after the death of Edward Somerset, fourth Earl of Worcester, in 1628, since Naunton writes that "as I have placed him last so was he the last liver of all." It was also probably written after 1632, the year of the death of Sir William Knollys, the Earl of Banbury. Banbury's name is included in the list of the sons of Sir Francis Knollys, and it is Naunton's practice not to mention any person still living who was involved in any of the court controversies that he describes—in this case the bitter feud between the Knollys family and the Norrises. The phrase, "since Earl of Banbury," used to describe Sir William, might be interpreted as an indication that the work was written before Sir William's death in May 1632; but Naunton uses the same phraseology in writing about Robert Cecil when it is definite that he is writing after Cecil's death, which he describes.

Naunton's reference to "the late compositions for Knighthood" is further evidence that the work was written after 1632, since it was in the years from 1630 to 1632 that the rule for enforced knighthood was revived by King Charles as a means of obtaining money for the crown.

Naunton mentions as "yet living" Lettice Knollys, who outlived three illustrious husbands—Walter Devereux, the first Earl of Es-

25

sex; Robert Dudley, the Earl of Leicester; and Sir Christopher Blount—and who died at ninety-four years of age in 1634. The *Fragmenta*, therefore, was written before that time.

The indicated date of composition, then, is 1633. In the first part of that year Naunton had given up active attendance at court because of increasing lameness. He was completely invalid in July and never recovered from the paralysis that set in.[1] As his correspondence indicates, however, his mind was still very active, and it seems probable that it was then that he recalled this period of his young manhood.

The Factual Basis

Naunton was not born until five years after Elizabeth was crowned Queen of England. His contacts with her court were slight and did not occur until the closing years of her reign. His "observations" for the most part, then, were not based upon personal knowledge. Even when writing about Walsingham and Burghley, two men whom he did meet, Naunton, some forty years after the event, does not recall any information from his own experience. His employment in the service of the Earl of Essex occurred ten years later than the meetings with Walsingham and Burghley, and Naunton's study of Essex is more comprehensive and alive than his studies of most of the other courtiers. It has been difficult, though, for any writer to dim the vivid figure of Essex.

Nearly half of the courtiers portrayed in the *Fragmenta* lived on into the reign of King James, the period when Naunton was active at the court. If Naunton did not know them personally, he was in a position to hear about them from persons who did, as well as to hear recollections of Elizabeth's time. He gives credit to these sources of information with the use of such phrases as "I know it from assured intelligence"; "I have heard it spoken"; "those that lived in his age, and from whence I have taken this little model of him"; "I have heard it from that party"; and "I have heard from a discreet man of his own."

Naunton credits two of his sources by name: Sir Walter Ralegh and Sir Henry Wotton. He cites the former in describing Elizabeth's lack of generosity in rewarding her soldiers and in commenting on the trial of Sir John Perrot. The source used in both cases is Ralegh's *History of the World,* which was published in 1614.[2] It is also probable that Naunton had passages from Ralegh's *Prerogative of Parliaments* in mind for the story of Carwarden, and for the brief discussion of impositions and the royal prerogative.[3]

Naunton acknowledges his dependence upon Wotton for information about the Earl of Essex. The source in this case is Wotton's *A Parallel between Robert, Late Earl of Essex, and George, Late Duke of Buckingham.*[4] Two of Naunton's observations about the rule of Elizabeth—her policy toward Spain and her spiritual aids— are similar to ideas expressed in Wotton's *State of Christendom,* which was written in 1594.[5] Wotton was active at King James's court at the same time as Naunton, and much of their official correspondence is recorded. It is likely that Naunton had his own manuscript copies of Wotton's works.

Naunton also made use of William Camden's *Annales Rerum Anglicarum et Hibernicarum Regnante Elizabetha* as a source. The complete Latin text of Camden's work was published in 1625. An English translation of the first three parts (from a French version) was published in 1627, and a complete translation in 1630. Naunton, with his university background, probably used the original Latin. In six passages of the *Fragmenta* Naunton follows Camden's text closely enough to indicate clearly his borrowing from it, but it is probable that he also used Camden for information found in other parts of the work.[6]

The Form and Style

Naunton's *Fragmenta Regalia* is a history of the first Queen Elizabeth's reign, told in the form of character studies. A series of observations about Elizabeth herself opens the *Fragmenta,* and this is followed by shorter portraits of twenty-two members of her court. The order of the work is generally chronological. Beginning with Elizabeth's lineage and her position during the reigns of Edward and Mary, Naunton continues with her accession to the throne and the change in religion. Throughout the rest of the work some of the principal events of the reign are touched upon. The order of the individual character studies is also chronological—the men are presented according to the time when they were most active at the court. Thus the sketches of Leicester, Sussex, and Burghley occur first, and the sketches of Ralegh, Essex, Cecil, and Worcester are toward the end. However, except for the most famous year of all, "Tilbury in eighty-eight,"[7] the work is without mention of dates.

The *Fragmenta* appears to be the first example of an English writer using a series of short character sketches to describe a period of history.[8] The form was afterward taken up by men writing about the reign of King James, principally Anthony Weldon in his *Court and Character of King James* (London, 1650) and Arthur Wilson in *The History of Great Britain, Being the Life and Reign of King James the First* (London, 1653). It was with Edward Hyde, the Earl of Clarendon, however, in his *History of the Rebellion* (published posthumously, 1702–4), that the full potentialities of the form were realized.

Naunton does not seem to have had any specific model upon which he based his work. Short individual character sketches of recently deceased nobility were in circulation in the decade or so before he wrote. The outstanding example is probably Francis Bacon's "In Felicem Memoriam Elizabethae, Angliae Reginae."[9] More immediate to the time of Naunton's work was Sir Henry Wotton's *Parallel between Robert, Late Earl of Essex, and George, Late Duke of Buckingham.* Naunton was well acquainted with this work and, in fact, used portions of it for his own study of the Earl of Essex. An earlier work, which the *Fragmenta* resembles more than any other, is John Clapham's *Elizabeth of England: Certain Observations concerning the Life and Reign of Queen Elizabeth,* written in 1603.[10] Clapham's work, as the title indicates, is more exclusively concerned with Elizabeth than Naunton's is, and there is a greater emphasis on the overall narrative. However, in one long digression, Clapham does present a study of Lord Burghley (who had been Clapham's employer) and in shorter digressions comments on Leicester, Hatton, Ralegh, and Essex. Clapham's work was not published in Naunton's time and apparently did not circulate in manuscript. There is no direct evidence that Naunton was acquainted with it, but some of the qualities that he observes in the Queen were also described by Clapham.

Another influence to be noted is that of the writers who followed the Theophrastan form—the portrayal of character types—which reached the apex of its popularity in the 1620s in the work of Joseph Hall, Sir Thomas Overbury, and John Earle. Their possible influence on the short biographical sketch of this period is obvious. However, Naunton is generally free of the fault of attempting to force his subjects into the rigid types used by many of the character writers and tries instead, although not always successfully, to portray the individuality of each of the courtiers. The outstanding exception to this occurs in the sketch of Sir Christopher Hatton, which, as a result, is the poorest of the lot. But then any character study of Hatton by Naunton was bound to turn out insultingly unfavorable due to Naunton's extreme antipathy to Hatton resulting from the quarrel between Hatton and Sir John Perrot, to whom Naunton was related by marriage. Compared to the best characters of the Overburian collection or to those of John Earle, Naunton's work lacks their penetrating and epigrammatic statement of character motivation. Instead, he uses the illustrative anecdote—the Lord of Leicester and the Gentleman Usher Bowyer, or Sir John Perrot in the "great chamber" at Dublin—or sometimes a mere biographical or genealogical account.

By Elizabethan standards, Naunton at seventy was a very old man when he wrote the *Fragmenta Regalia.* And signs of old age are evident in his writing—in its repetitiousness and in its obscurity. He twice tells the story of Mountjoy stealing away into Brittany and uses the same epigram to describe Sir Francis Vere that he used to close his sketch of Sir Philip Sidney. Naunton's vague references—Elizabeth's "one stain, or taint," and her "aversion to grant Tyrone the least drop of her mercy"—were probably clearer to the readers of the seventeenth century than to those of the twentieth. One wonders, however, if the meaning of Leicester's "play" being "chiefly at the foregame" was not rather obscure even at the time it was written.

Naunton's use of the decorative Latin phrase in his writing represents the observation of a stylistic convention of his time, and his employment of the device is not excessive in comparison with its use by such of his contemporaries as Bacon and Wotton. It is, incidentally, a trait observable in Naunton's correspondence throughout his career.

The sense of life that Naunton is able to realize in recounting his anecdotes is remarkable. Much of the effect is the result of his use of select detail and of direct quotation: "God's death, my lord," says Elizabeth as she reproves the Earl of Leicester. "Fail you not to come to court," she tells the sweet-faced young Charles Blount. "I perceive every fool must have a favor," the Earl of Essex taunts Mountjoy, and the courtiers whisper about the same story.

Naunton's use of metaphor is also sometimes striking. The continuous military campaigns in the Netherlands during Elizabeth's reign are the "Queen's seminaries and nurseries of many brave soldiers," indicating the necessary part that they played not only in maintaining the Queen's forces but also in the education of the young nobility. The description of Essex as one who "drew in too fast like a child sucking a uberous breast," suggests the impatient ambition of the man and the strangeness of the relationship between Essex and the Queen in view of the disparity of their ages.

3
The Text of the *Fragmenta Regalia*

The Early Editions

The *Fragmenta Regalia* was not printed until 1641, six years after Sir Robert Naunton's death. Five editions then appeared, the latest in 1653. The two editions appearing in 1641 were apparently based on corrupt copies of the text, and little care was taken to improve them. Omissions occur in both editions, as well as numerous literal errors that appear to be the result of carelessness on the part of the compositor in both the reading and the setting of the copy. The names of the printers do not appear in the first three editions. The first of these, 1641(A), has the device of a peacock on the title page.[1] The head ornament on the first page of the text (Sig. A2^r) is reproduced by Henry Plomer in *English Printer's Ornaments* (London, 1924), plate 53, where it is described as "spirals of foliage" with "national emblems: lion and unicorn." Plomer identifies it as belonging to the Eliot's Court Press and as being in use between 1606 and 1644.[2] The printers of this press who were active in 1641 were Edward Griffin and Elizabeth Purslowe.[3] The collation of the 1641(A) text with that of the 1641(B) edition and with manuscript copies of the work shows six omissions of approximately one line each as well as shorter omissions of individual words and phrases.

The 1641(B) edition was the work of a different printer. The device on the title page is reproduced in plate 126 of Plomer's *Ornaments.* Plomer describes it as an "arabesque ornament," and identifies it as having belonged to Edward Allde. Allde is believed to have died in 1628, and his business was carried on by his widow, Elizabeth, until 1640. At that date she turned over her copyrights to Richard Oulton, who had married one of her daughters.[4] Oulton was active in the printing trade until 1643,[5] so it seems probable

31

that the 1641(B) edition was from his press. The collation of the text of this edition with the 1641(A) edition and manuscript copies of the work shows fourteen short omissions and an unusually large number of literal errors. Incorrect pagination is an additional indication of the generally poor workmanship in the setting up of this edition.

The 1642 edition (W. 251) is from the press of the same printer who printed the 1641(A) edition. The title page devices and the head ornaments are identical. The text is also from the 1641(A) edition and has the same omissions. The few changes made do not indicate that there was any reference to the original copy. Misreadings that could have been corrected by such references are retained.[6]

The 1650 edition (W. 252) of the *Fragmenta* is a revision based on the 1642 text. The same omissions occur as in the earlier edition, but many of the literal errors are corrected. It is apparent from the nature of the corrections that a manuscript copy of the text was used for this purpose. This revised 1650 text was also employed for the 1653 edition with only a few changes. The changes are of an independent nature and do not correspond to readings found in any of the other copies of the work.

The examination of these early editions of the *Fragmenta Regalia* shows, then, three distinct versions of the text, with two of these being closely related. One version is that of the 1641(B) edition, which is based on a copy different from all the other editions. Another is the 1641(A) text, and it was used (with a few minor changes) for the 1642 edition. The third version is the revised form of the 1642 text used for the 1650 and 1653 editions.[7] None of these presents a good text of Naunton's work. The copies used for the bases of these editions were apparently without authority. Faulty readings common to many of the manuscript copies of the work are present. The omissions mentioned above occur in all of the editions. Literal errors are present and words are omitted even in the revised editions and in many cases affect the meaning of the passages in which they occur.

The Later Editions

1. **1694.** *Arcana Aulica: or Walsingham's Manual . . . To which is added Fragmenta Regalia; or Observations on Queen Elizabeth,*

Her Times, and Favorites. By Sir Robert Naunton. London: for Matthew Gillyflower, 1694. 157–247. The text of the 1650 edition, but with a few readings taken from the edition of 1653.

2. (A) **1707.** *The Phenix; or, A Revival of Scarce and Valuable Pieces . . . By a Gentleman Who Has Made It His Business to Search after Such Pieces for Twenty Years Past.* London: for I. Morphew, 1707. 1 : 181–221. The text of the 1641(A) edition with a few emendations.

(B) **1721.** *A Collection of Choice, Scarce, and Valuable Tracts . . . By a Gentleman Who Has Search'd after Them for Above Twenty Years.* London: for D. Browne, 1721. A reissue of *The Phenix.*

3. **1744.** *The Harleian Miscellany; or, A Collection of Scarce, Curious, and Entertaining Pamphlets and Tracts . . .* [First edition]. London: for T. Osborne, 1744–46. 2 : 72–95.

1810. *The Harleian Miscellany . . .* [Second edition]. London: for R. Dutton, 1808–11. 5 : 121–55.

1809. *The Harleian Miscellany . . .* [Third edition]. London: for John White, 1808–13. 2 : 81–108. The text of the 1641(B) edition with some silent emendations. Additional emendations are given as footnotes without changing the text.

4. **1750.** *Somers Tracts: A Collection of Scarce and Valuable Tracts . . .* [First edition]. London: for F. Cogan, 1748–52. 5 [second collection, 2]:350–83.

1809. *Somers Tracts.* The second edition, revised, augmented, and arranged by Walter Scott, Esq. London, 1809–15. 1 : 251–83. The text of the 1641(B) edition.

5. **1797.** *"Paul Hentzner's Travels in England" . . . To Which Is Now Added, Sir Robert Naunton's "Fragmenta Regalia" . . .* London: for Edward Jeffery, 1797. 77–152. The text of the 1641(B) edition as it appears in *The Harleian Miscellany* (see Item 3 above). To this the following is added at the end as part of the text: "Lord Herbert / The accomplished, the brave, and romantic Lord Her-

bert of Cherbury, was born in this reign, and laid the foundation of that admirable learning of which he was afterwards complete master."

6. 1808. *"Memoirs of Robert Cary"* . . . *and "Fragmenta Regalia"; Being a History of Queen Elizabeth's Favorites.* By Sir Robert Naunton. Edinburgh: for A. Constable, 1808. 169–301. The text of the 1642 edition with a few emendations.

7. 1814. *"The Court of Queen Elizabeth": Originally Written by Sir Robert Naunton, under the title "Fragmenta Regalia."* With considerable biographical addition by James Caulfield. London, for G. Smeeton, 1814. The text of the 1641(B) edition, partially rewritten by the editor. It includes some faulty emendations.

8. 1824. *Fragmenta Regalia: Memoirs of Elizabeth, Her Court and Favorites.* By Sir Robert Naunton, Secretary of State to King James the First. London: for Charles Baldwyn, 1824. The text of the 1641(B) edition, extensively emended by reference to the British Library manuscripts. Unfortunately, the edition has no textual annotatons, and some of the emendations, partly unnecessary, appear to have been made independently by the editor. S. A. Allibone, in the article on Naunton in his *Dictionary of Authors* (Philadelphia, 1870), lists the editor as P. W. Dodd.

9. 1870. *English Reprints: Sir Robert Naunton, "Fragmenta Regalia."* Reprinted from the third posthumous edition of 1653 by Edward Arber. London, 1870. The text of the 1653 edition with some unnoted emendation. This was the fifth edition, not the third as stated by Arber.

10. 1889. *Sir Robert Naunton's Fragmenta Regalia.* Cassell's National Library. Vol. 165. Based on the 1641(B) edition.

11. 1927. *A Miscellany of Tracts and Pamphlets.* Edited by A. C. Ward. Oxford, 1927. 159–221. The text of the Arber edition.

The Text of the Present Edition

Naunton's *Fragmenta Regalia* circulated widely in manuscript form as well as in the printed editions. Many of the manuscript copies are still extant in both public and private collections. Unfortunately, the existence of the manuscripts does not in itself mean that all or any of them originated before the work was published. This is made clear in the preface to the edition of the *Fragmenta* published in 1694, forty-one years after the previous edition:

> As for Sir Robert Naunton's *Fragmenta,* I shall say no more of them, to the reputation that they have in the world, than that they have been highly esteemed, as an authentic collection of curious remarks, by the generality of men of place and business: insomuch, that since the book was out of print, it has been the constant work of diverse clerks in parliament, and term-time, to transcribe copies of it for the use and service of the lovers of antiquities and state history; and these copies had the honor afterward to be treasured up among the choicest manuscripts.[8]

In the preparation of the present edition, twenty-two manuscripts were examined.[9] In these it appears that the scribes were more intent on turning out a fast piece of work than a careful one. In most of the manuscripts the work is divided between two or even three hands. The presence of corrupt passages common to the majority of the manuscripts seems to indicate that the text was carelessly handled at an early date. Only two of these manuscripts are dated, Folger MS. G. a. 11, 1638, and Folger MS. G. b. 21, 1640. Both of these precede the first printed editions of 1641. Listings in the reports of the *Historical Manuscripts Commission* of copies in private collections do not describe any of them as being dated or in any way authoritative.

The text chosen for the present edition is taken from the earliest of the dated manuscripts, Folger MS. G. a. 11. It is a bound paper quarto measuring 18.3 by 13.2 centimeters. It consists of thirty-three leaves bound in blue paper boards. The earliest record of this manuscript is a listing (as item 228) in a catalog of Thomas Thorpe, the London bookseller, in 1835. It was listed again in a supplementary catalog (as item 216) in 1836, at which time it was sold to Sir Thomas Phillipps.[10] The manuscript remained in the Phillipps Collection (as MS. 10134) until 1895, when it was sold to the dealer Tregaskis. It is assumed that Mr. Folger purchased the manuscript from Tregaskis, since the price paid for it corresponds to a listing taken from a Tregaskis catalog.

The collation of the *Fragmenta* text of Folger MS. G. a. 11 with other manuscript copies and the printed editions shows several short omissions and some literal errors. As a basis for emendation, two other Folger manuscripts, G. b. 21 and G. b. 20, were used. The first of these, MS. G. b. 21, is dated 1640 in the hand of the scribe. Unfortunately, the text of this manuscript is badly truncated. Many long passages are completely omitted, and others are shortened through the use of paraphrase. Because of this it has been necessary in some cases to refer to one of the undated manuscripts. Folger MS. G. b. 20 was chosen for this purpose. This manuscript is part of a collection of letters and papers of Sir Nathaniel Bacon. Since the other items in this collection are dated from 1570 to 1640, it seems probable that the provenance of this *Fragmenta* manuscript was contemporary with that of the other two manuscripts used.

In the transcription of the text, catchwords have been omitted and scribal abbreviations have been expanded. The manuscript contains some corrections made in what appears to be the original hand; these have been accepted without notice. All other variations from the Folger MS. G. a. 11 text are noted.

∽∽∽∽∽∽∽∽∽∽∽∽∽∽∽∽∽∽∽

Fragmenta Regalia
or observations on Queen Elizabeth
her Times & Favorites

	1. Leicester.	1. Sussex.
	2. Cecil, senior.	2. Sidney.
	3. Walsingham.	3. Willoughby.
	4. Bacon.	
	5. Knowles.	4. Norris.
Togati	6. Hatton.	5. Nottingham. *De Militia*
	7. Pakington.	6. Perrot.
	8. Hunsdon.	7. Ralegh.
	9. Greville.	8. Essex.
	10. Buckhurst.	9. Montjoy.
	11. Cecil, junior.	10. Vere.
	12. Worcester.	

Anno Domini
1638
FORMAT OF THE TITLE PAGE OF FOLGER MS. G. A. 11

4
Fragmenta Regalia
or
Observations on Queen Elizabeth, Her Times & Favorites

To take her in the original, she was daughter of Henry the Eighth by Anne Boleyn, his second of six wives which he had, one of the maids of honor to the divorced Queen Catherine of Austria, or (as they now style it) Infanta of Spain, and from thence taken into the royal bed.[1]

That she was of a most noble and royal extract by her father will not fall into question, for on that side there was disembogued into her veins by a confluence of blood the very abstract of all the greatest houses in Christendom.[2] And remarkable it is, considering the violent desertion of the royal houses of the Britains by the invasion of the Saxons and afterwards by the conquest of the Normans, that by the vicissitude of times and through the discontinuance for almost a thousand years, the regal scepter should fall back into the current of the old British blood in the person of her renowned grandfather Henry the Seventh, together with whatsoever the German, Norman, Burgundian, Castilian, and French achievements with the intermarriages, which eight hundred years had acquired, incorporated, and brought back into the old regal line.

By her mother she was of no sovereign descent yet noble and very ancient in the family of Boleyn though some erroneously brand it with a citizen's rise or original, which was yet but of a second brother,[3] who, as it were, divining the greatness and luster

37

to come to his house, was sent to the city to acquire wealth *ad aedificandam antiquam domum.*[4] Unto whose achievements (for he was Lord Mayor of London) fell in as it was averred both the blood and inheritance of the eldest brother for want of issue male. By which accumulation[5] the house within few descents mounted *in culmen honoris* and was suddenly elated into the best families of England and Ireland, as Howard, Ormond, Sackville, and diverse others.

Having thus touched and now leaving her stirp, I come to her person and as she came to the crown by the decease of her brother and sister. Under Edward she was his and one of the darlings of fortune, for besides the consideration of blood there was between these two princes a concurrence and sympathy in their natures and affections together with that celestial bond,[6] conformity in religion, which made them one. For the King ever called her his dearest and sweetest sister and was scarce his own man she being absent, which was not so between him and his sister the Lady Mary.

Under her sister she found her condition much altered, for it was resolved and her destiny decreed to set her an apprentice in the school of affliction and to draw her through that ordeal fire of trial, the better to mold and fashion her to rule and sovereignty. Which finished, fortune, calling to mind that the time of her servitude was expired, gave up her indenture and therewithal delivered into her custody a scepter as the reward of her service. Which was about the twenty-sixth year of her age, a time in which as for her externals she was full blown, so was she for her internals grown up and seasoned by adversity in the exercise of her virtues, for it seems fortune meant no more than to show her a piece of her variety and changeableness of her nature and so to conduct her to her destined felicity.

She was of personage tall, of hair and complexion fair, and therewithal well favored, but high-nosed, of limbs and feature neat.[7] And (which added to the luster of these exterior graces) of a stately and majestic comportment, participating of this more of her father than of her mother, who was of an inferior alloy, plausible and, as the French word hath it, more debonaire, and affable, virtues which might well suit with majesty and which descending as

QUEEN ELIZABETH

hereditary to the daughter did render her of a more sweet temper and endear her more to the love and liking of the people, who gave her the name and fame of a most gracious and popular prince, the atrocity of her father's nature being allayed in hers by her mother's sweet inclination, for to take no more than the character out of his own mouth, "He never spared any man in his anger, nor woman in his lust."

If we search farther into her intellectuals and ability, the whole course of her government deciphers them to admiration of her posterity, for it was full of magnanimity tempered with justice, pity, and piety, and (to speak truly) noted but with one stain or taint,[8] all her deprivations either of life or liberty being legal and necessitated.

She was learned (her sex and her times considered) beyond all common belief, for letters about this time and somewhat before began to be of esteem and fashion, the former ages being overcast with the mists and fogs of the Roman ignorance, and it was the maxim that overruled the foregoing times that ignorance was the mother of devotion.

Her wars were a long time more in auxiliary parts in assisting foreign princes and states than by invasion of any, till common policy advised it for a safer way to strike first and abroad than at home to expect wars, in all which she was felicious and victorious.

The change and alteration of religion upon the instant of her accession (the smoke and fire of her sister's martyrdoms scarce quenched) was none of her least remarkable actions. But the support and establishment thereof with the means of her subsistence amidst so many powerful enemies abroad and those many domestic practices were (methinks) works of inspiration and of no human providence, which at her sister's departure she most religiously acknowledged, ascribing the glory of her deliverance to God alone. For she being then at Hatfield and under a guard and the Parliament then sitting, she received the news both of the Queen's death and of her own proclamation by the general consent of the house and public suffrage of the people, whereat falling on her knees, after a good time of respiration, she uttered this verse of the Psalm, *A domino factum est illud, et est mirabile in oculis meis*, which we find to this day on the stamp of her gold, with this on her silver, *Posui Deum adjutorem meum.*[9]

Her ministers and instruments of state, such as were *participes curarum*[10] and bore a great part of the burden, were many, and those memorable. But they were only favorites not minions, such as acted more by her own princely rules and judgment than by their own will and appetites; which she observed to the last, for we find no Gaveston, Vere, or Spencer[11] to have swayed alone during forty-four years. Which was a well settled and advised maxim, for it valued her the more, it awed the most secure, it took best with the people, and it staved off all emulations which are apt to rise and vent in obloquious acrimony, even against the prince, where there is only admitted into these high administrations a *major palatii.*[12]

The principal note of her reign will be that she ruled much by faction and parties,[13] which she herself both made, upheld, and weakened as her own great judgment advised, for I disassent from the common and received opinion that my Lord of Leicester was absolute and alone in her grace and favor. And though I come somewhat short of the knowledge of those times and shoot at random, I know from assured intelligence that it was not so, for proof whereof (amongst many that I could name) I will both relate a story and therein a known truth.

Bowyer, a Gentleman of the Black Rod,[14] being charged by express command to look precisely to all admissions into the privy chamber, one day stayed a very great captain (and a follower of my Lord of Leicester) from entrance, for that he was neither very well known nor a sworn servant to the Queen. At which repulse, the gentleman, bearing high on my lord's favor, told him that he might perchance procure him a discharge. Leicester coming to the contestation said publicly (which was none of his wont) that he was a knave and should not continue long in his office, and so turning about to go into the Queen. Bowyer, who was a bold gentleman and well beloved, stepped in before him and fell at Her Majesty's feet, relates the story and humbly craves Her Grace's pleasure and whether my Lord of Leicester were king or Her Majesty queen. Whereunto she replied with her wonted oath, "God's death, my lord, I have wished you well, but my favor is not locked up for you that others shall not partake thereof, for I have many servants unto whom I have and will at my pleasure bequeath my favors and likewise reassume the same, and if you think to rule here, I will take a course to see you forthcoming. I will have here but one mistress and no master, and look that no ill happen to him lest it be severely required at your hands." Which so quelled my lord that his feigned humility was long after one of his best virtues.

Moreover, Thomas, Earl of Sussex, then Lord Chamberlain, was one of his professed antagonists to his dying day. And for my Lord of Hunsdon and Sir Thomas Sackville, after Lord Treasurer, who were all contemporaries, he was wont to say of them that they were all of the Tribe of Dan[15] and were *noli me tangere*,[16] implying that they were not to be contested with, for they were indeed of the Queen's near kindred.

From whence, and in many more instances, I conclude that she was absolute and sovereign mistress of her grace and that those to whom she distributed her favors were never more than tenants at will and stood on no better ground than her princely pleasure and their own good behavior.

And this I present as a known observation, that she was, though[17] very capable of counsel, absolute enough in her own resolutions, which was ever apparent even to her last and in that of her stiff aversion to grant Tyrone the least drop of her mercy[18] though earnestly and frequently advised, yea, wrought on, by her own council of state with many pressing reasons and (as the state of the kingdom then stood, I may speak with assurance) necessitating arguments.

If we look into her inclination as it was disposed either to munificence or frugality, we shall find in them many notable observations, for all her dispensations were so poised as though discretion and justice had both agreed to stand at the beam and see them weighed out in due proportion, the maturity of her years and judgment meeting in concurrence, and at such an age as seldom lapseth to excess.

To consider them apart, we have not many precedents of her liberality or of any large donatives to particular men, my Lord of Essex his book of parks[19] excepted, which was a princely gift, and some few more of a lesser size to my Lord of Leicester, Hatton, and others. Her rewards consisted chiefly in grants of leases, of offices, and places of judicature, but for ready money and in any great sums she was very sparing; which we may guess was partly a virtue drawn rather out of necessity than nature, for she had many layings out, and as her wars were lasting so their charge increased to her last period. And I am of opinion with Sir Walter Ralegh[20] that those brave men of her times and of the militia tasted little more of her bounty than her grace and good words with their due entertainment, for she ever paid the soldier well, which was the honor of her[21] time and more than ever her great adversary of Spain could do. So that when we come to the consideration of her frugality, the observation will be little more than this: that her bounty and it were so woven together that the one was stinted by an honorable way of spending and the other limited by a necessitated way of sparing.

The Irish action we may call a malady and a consumption of her times, for it accompanied her to her end, and it was of so profuse and vast expense that it drew near a distemperature of state and passion in herself. For towards her last she grew somewhat hard to please, her armies being accustomed to prosperity and the Irish prosecution not answering her expectation and her wonted success, for it was a good while an unthrifty and inauspicious war which did much disturb and mislead her judgment. And the more for that it was a precedent which was taken out of her own pattern: for as the Queen by way of diversion had at her coming to the crown supported the revolted states of Holland, so did the King of Spain return the trick on herself towards her going out by cherishing the Irish rebellion.

Where it falls into consideration what the estate of the kingdom and the crown revenues were then able to endure and embrace. If we look into the establishment of those times with the list of the Irish army (omitting the defeatures at Blackwater with all precedent expenses as it stood from my Lord of Essex' undertaking to[22] the surrender of Kinsale under the General Mountjoy and somewhat after), we shall find the horse and foot troops were for three or four years together much about 20,000 pounds, besides the naval charge which was a dependent of the same war in that the Queen was then enforced to keep in continual pay a strong fleet at sea to attend the Spanish coast and ports, both to alarm[23] the Spaniards and to intercept his forces designed for the Irish assistance. So that the charge of that war alone did cost the Queen 300,000 pounds per annum, which was not the moiety of her other disbursements: an expense which without the public aids the state and[24] royal receipts could not much longer have endured, which out of her own frequent letters and complaints to the Deputy Mountjoy for cashiering part of that list as soon as he could may be collected, for the Queen was then driven to a strait.

We are naturally prone to applaud the times behind us and to vilify the present, for the current of fame carries it to this day how regally and victoriously she lived and died without the grievance or grudge of her people. Yet the truth may appear without retraction from the honor of so great a prince. It is manifest, she left more debts unpaid, taken up upon the credit of her privy seals, than her progenitors did or could have taken up that were in a hundred years before her,[25] which was an enforced piece of state: to lay the burden on that horse which was best able to bear it at the dead lift when neither her receipts could yield her relief at the pinch nor the urgency of her affairs endure the delays of parliamentary assistance. And for such aids it is likewise apparent that she received more, and that with the love of her people, than any two of her predecessors that took most, which was a fortune strained out of her subjects through the plausibility of her comportment and (as I would say without offense) the prodigal distribution of her grace to all sorts of subjects. For I believe no prince living that was so tender of honor and so exactly stood for the preservation of sovereignty, that was so great a courter of her people, yea, of the commons, and that stooped and descended lower in presenting her person to the public view as she passed in her progresses and perambulations and in the ejaculations of her prayers upon the people.

And truly, though much may be given in praise of her providence and good husbandry and that she could on all good occasions abate her magnanimity and therewithal comply with her parliaments and for all that come off at last with honor, yet must we ascribe some part of her commendation to the wisdom of the times and the choice of parliament men. For I find not that they were at any time given to any violent or pertinacious dispute, the elections being made of grave and discreet persons not factious and ambitious of fame, such as came not to the house with a malevolent spirit of contention but with a preparation to consult on the public good, rather to comply than to contest with majesty.

Neither do I find that the house was weakened and pestered through the admission of too many young heads as it hath been of later times. Which remembers me of the Recorder Martin's speech[26] about the tenth of our late sovereign lord King James, when there were accounts taken of forty gentlemen not above twenty and some not exceeding sixteen years, which made him say that it was the ancient custom for old men to make laws for young ones, but that then he saw the case altered and that there were children elected into the great council of our kingdom which came to invade and invert nature and to enact laws to govern their fathers. Sure we are, the house took the common cause into their consideration, and they saw the Queen had many times just occasion and need enough to use their assistance. Neither do I remember that the house did ever capitulate or prefer their private to the public and Queen's necessities but waited their times and in the first place gave their supply and according to the exigency of her affairs, but failed not at last to obtain what they desired, so that the Queen and her parliaments had ever good fortune to depart in love and reciprocal terms, which are considerations that have not been so exactly observed in our late assemblies as I would to God they had been. For considering the great debts left on the King and into what encumbrances the house itself had then drawn him, His Majesty was not well used, though I lay not the blame on the whole suffrage of the house, where he had many good friends. But I dare avouch it, had the house been freed of half a dozen of popular and discontented persons, such as with the fellow that burnt the Temple of Ephesus would be talked of though but for doing of mischief,[27] I am confident the King had obtained that which in reason and at his first accession he ought to have received freely and without condition.

But pardon this digression which is here remembered not in the way of aggravation but in true zeal to the public good and presented in a caveat to future times, for I am not ignorant how the genius and spirit of the kingdom now moves to make His Majesty[28] amends on any occasion and how desirous the subject is to expiate that offense at any rate. May it please His Majesty graciously to make trial of his subjects' affections and at what price they now value his goodness and magnanimity.

But to the purpose. The Queen was not ignorant[29] that as the strength of the kingdom consisted in the multitude of subjects so the security of her person consisted and rested in the love and fidelity of her people, which she politically affected as hath been thought somewhat beneath the height of her spirit and magnanimity.

Moreover, it will be a true note of her providence that she would always listen to her profit, for she would not refuse the information of mean persons which proposed improvement, and had learned the philosophy of *hoc agere,* to look unto her own work.

Of the which, there is a notable example of one Carwarden, an under officer of the customhouse,[30] who observing his time presented her with a paper showing her how she was abused in the renting of the customs, and therewithal humbly desired Her Majesty to conceal him for that it did concern two or three of her greatest councillors whom customer Smith[31] had bribed with 2,000 pounds a man so to lose the Queen 20,000 pounds per annum. Which being made known to the lords, they gave strict charge that Carwarden should not have access to the back stairs, till at last Her Majesty smelling the craft and missing Carwarden, she sent for him, backed and encouraged him to stand to his information, which the poor man did so handsomely that within ten years he brought Smith to double his rent and to leave the customs to new farmers. So that we may take this also into observation that there were of the Queen's council which were not of the catalog of saints.[32]

Now as we have taken a view of some particular notions of her times, her nature, and necessities, it is not without the text to give a short note on the helps and advantages of her reign, which were without parallel, for she had neither husband, brother, sister, nor children to provide for, who as they are dependents on the crown so they necessarily draw livelihood from thence and do oftentimes exhaust and draw deep, especially when there is an ample fraternity royal and of princes of the blood as it was in the time of Edward the Third and Henry the Fourth; for when the crown cannot, the public ought to give them honorable allowance, for they are the honor and hopes of the kingdom, and the public which enjoys them hath the like honor with the father which begat them. And our common law which is the inheritance of the kingdom did ever of old provide aids for the primogenitus and eldest daughter. So that the multiplicity of courts and the great charge which necessarily follows a king, a queen, a prince, and a royal issue was a thing which was not *in rerum natura* during the space of forty-four years, and by time was worn out of memory and without the consideration of the present times, insomuch that the aids given for the late and right noble Prince Henry and to his sister, the Lady Elizabeth, were at first generally received as impositions of a new coining.[33] Yea, the late compositions for knighthood (though an ancient law)[34] fell also into the imputation of novelty for that it lay long covered in the embers of division between the houses of York and Lancaster and forgotten or connived at by the succeeding princes. So that the strangeness of the observation and difference of these latter reigns is that the Queen took up much beyond the power of laws which fell not into the murmur of the people, and her successors nothing but by the warrant of the law which nevertheless was conceived, through disuse, to be injurious to the liberty of the kingdom.

Now before I come to any further mention of her favorites (for hitherto I have delivered but some obvious passages thereby to prepare and smooth the way for the rest that follows), it is necessary that I touch on the relics of the other's reign. I mean on the body of her sister's council of state, which she retained entire, neither removing nor discontenting any although she knew them averse to her religion and in her sister's time perverse to her person, and private during all her troubles and imprisonment,[35] a prudence which was incompatible with her sister's nature, for she both dissipated and persecuted the major part of her brother's council. But this will be of certainty, that how compliable and obsequious so be she then found them, yet for a good space she made little use of their counsels more than in the ordinary course of the board, for she had a dormant table in her own princely breast. Yet she kept them together and in their places without any sudden change so that we may say of them, they were then of the court not of the council. For while she amused them by a kind of permissive disputation concerning the points controverted by both churches, she did set down her own gists[36] without their privity and made all her progressions *gradatim* but so that the tents of her secrets with the intent of their establishments were pitched before it was known where the court would sit down.

Neither do I find that any of her sister's council of state were either repugnant to her religion or opposed to her doings (Englefield, Master of Wards,[37] excepted, who withdrew himself from the board and shortly after from her dominions), so pliable and obedient they were to change with the times and their prince.

And of them there will fall a relation of recreation. Paulet, Marquess of Winchester and Lord Treasurer of England,[38] had served then four princes in as various times and changeable seasons that I may well say no time nor age hath yielded the like precedent. This man being noted to grow high in her favor as his place and experience required was questioned by an intimate friend of his how he stood for thirty years together amidst the changes and ruins of so many counselors and great personalities. "Why," quoth the Marquess, "*ortus sum ex salice non ex quercu.* I was made of the pliable willow, not of the oak."

And truly it seems the old man had taught them all, especially William, Earl of Pembroke,[39] for they two were always in the King's religion and ever zealous professors. Of these it is said that being both younger brothers yet of noble houses, they spent what was left them and came on trust to the court, where upon the bare stock of their wits they began to traffic for themselves, and prospered so well that they got, spent, and left more than any subjects from the Norman conquest to their own times. Whereupon it hath been prettily replied that they lived in a time of dissolution.

To conclude then of any of the former reign, it is said that these two lived and died in her grace and favor. The latter, upon his son's marriage with the Lady Catherine Grey,[40] was like utterly to have lost himself; but at the instant of the consummation, apprehending the unsafety and danger of an intermarriage with the blood royal, he fell at the Queen's feet, where he both acknowledged his presumption with tears and projected the cause and the divorce together. And so quick was he at his work, for it stood him upon, that upon the repudiation of the lady, he clapt up a marriage for his son the Lord Herbert with Mary Sidney, daughter to Sir Henry Sidney, then Lord Deputy of Ireland, the blow falling on Edward, late Earl of Hertford, who to his cost took up the divorced lady, of whom the Lord Beauchamp was born, and William, now Earl of Hertford, is descended.

I come now to present those of her own election, which she either admitted to her secrets of state or took into her grace and favor. Of whom in their order I crave leave to give unto posterity a cautious description with a short character and draft of the persons themselves; for without offense to others, I would be true to myself, their memories and merits, distinguishing those of the *militia* from the *togati,* and of both these she had as many and those as able ministers as any of her progenitors.

1. Leicester

It will be out of doubt that my Lord of Leicester was one of the first, whom she made Master of the Horse.[41] He was the youngest

ROBERT DUDLEY, EARL OF LEICESTER

son then living of the Duke of Northumberland,[42] beheaded *primo Mariae*. And his father was that Dudley which our histories couple with Empson,[43] and both so much infamed for the caterpillars of the commonwealth during the reign of Henry the Seventh. Who being of a noble extract was executed the first of Henry the Eighth, but not thereby so extinct but that he left a plentiful estate and such a son, who (as the vulgar speak) would live without a teat, for out of the ashes of his father's infamy he rose to be a duke and as high as subjection could permit or sovereignty endure. And though he could not find out any palliation to assume the crown in his own person, yet he projected and very nearly effected it by his son Gilford and by intermarriage with the Lady Jane Grey, and so by that way to bring it about into his loins. Observations which though they be beyond us and seem impertinent to the text, yet are they not much extravagant for they must lead and show us how the after passages were brought about with the dependencies on the hinges of a collateral workmanship.

And surely it will amaze a well settled judgment to look back at these times and to consider how this duke[44] could attain to such a pitch of greatness, his father dying in ignominy and at the gallows, his estate confiscate, and that for pilling and polling[45] of the people. But when we better think about it, we find that he was given up a sacrifice to appease the people, not for any offense committed against the person of the King;[46] so that in the matter he was a martyr for the prerogative, and the King in honor could do no less than give back to his son the privilege of his blood with the acquiring of his father's profession, for he was a lawyer and of the King's Council at Law before he came to be *ex interioribus conciliis,* where besides the licking of his own fingers he got the King a mass of riches, and that not with the hazard but with the loss of his life and fame for the King's father's sake.

Certain it is that this son was left rich in purse and brain, which are good foundations and fuel[47] to ambition, and it may be supposed he was on all occasions well heard of the King as a person of mark and of compassion in his eye. But I find not that he did put up for advancement in Henry the Eighth his time, although a vast aspirer and provident storer. It seems he thought the King's reign was much given to the falling sickness.[48] But espying his time fitting and the sovereignty in the hands of a pupil prince, he thought he might then put up as well for it as the best; for having the possession of blood, and a purse, with a headpiece of vast extent, he soon got honor, and no sooner there but he began to side it with the best, even with the Protector,[49] and in the conclusion got his and his brother's heads,[50] still aspiring till he expired in the loss of his own. So that posterity may by reading the father and grandfather make judgment of the son, for we shall find this Robert, whose original we have now traced the better to present him, was inheritor of the genius and craft of his father, and Ambrose of the estate,[51] of whom hereafter we shall make some short mention.

We take him now as he was admitted into the court and Queen's favor. And here he was not to seek to play his part well and dexterously, but his play was chiefly at the foregame, not that he was a learner at the after game, but that he loved not the after wit;[52] for they report, and not unjustly, that he was seldom behind hand[53] with his gamesters and that they always went with the loss.

He was a very goodly person: tall and singularly well featured, and all his youth wellfavored of a sweet aspect, but high-foreheaded, which (as I should take it) was of no discommendation; but toward his latter end, which with old men was but a middle age, he grew high colored and red faced. So that the Queen in this had much of her father, and excepting some of her kindred and some few that had handsome wits in crooked bodies,[54] she always took personage in the way of election,[55] for the people have it to this day in a proverb, "King Henry loved a man." Being thus in her grace, she called to mind the sufferings of his ancestors both in her father's and sister's reign and restored his and his brother's blood, creating Ambrose, the elder, Earl of Warwick and himself Earl of Leicester. And as he was *ex primitiis*, or of her first choice, so he rested not there but long enjoyed her favor and therewith much what he listed till time and emulation (the companions of greatness) had resolved of her period and to cover him at his setting in a cloud at Cornbury, not by so violent a death and by the fatal sentence of judicature as that of his father's and grandfather's was, but (as it was suggested)[56] by that poison which he had prepared for others, wherein they report him a rare artist. I am not bound to give credit to all vulgar relations or to the libels of his times,[57] which are commonly forced and falsified suitable to the moods and humors of men in passion and discontent. But that which leads me to think him no good man is (amongst other things of known truth) that of my Lord of Essex his death in Ireland and the marriage of his lady, yet living,[58] which I forbear to press in regard he is long since dead and others living whom it may concern.

To take him in the observation of his letters and writings (which should best set him off), for such as have fallen into my hands, I never yet saw a style and phrase more seemingly religious and fuller of the strains of devotion, and were they not sincere I should doubt much of his well-being, and I fear he was too well seen in the aphorisms and principles of Nicholas the Florentine and in the reaches of Caesar Borgia.[59]

And hitherto I have only touched him in his courtship, I conclude him in his lance. He was sent governor by the Queen to the revolted states of Holland, where we read not of his wonders, for (as they say) he had more of Mercury than of Mars, and that his device might have been without prejudice to the great Caesar: *Veni, vidi, redivi.*[60]

2. Sussex

His corrival before mentioned was Thomas Radcliffe, Earl of Sussex,[61] who in his constellation was his direct opposite, for he

THOMAS RADCLIFFE, EARL OF SUSSEX

was indeed one of the Queen's martialists and did her very good service in Ireland at her first accession till she recalled him to the court, where she made him Lord Chamberlain.

But he played not his game with the cunning and dexterity that Leicester did, which was much the more facete courtier though Sussex was thought the honester man and far the better soldier but he lay too open on his guard.

He was a goodly gentleman and of a brave and noble nature, true and constant to his friends[62] and servants. He was also of a very ancient and noble lineage honored through many descents by the title of Viscount Fitzwalters.

Moreover, there was such an antipathy in his nature to that of Leicester's that being together in court and both in high employments, they grew to a direct feud and both in continual oppositions, the one setting the watch and the other the sentinel, each on other's actions and motions. For my Lord of Sussex was of a great spirit which, backed with the Queen's special favor and supported by a great and ancient inheritance, could not brook the other's empire. Insomuch that the Queen upon sundry occasions had somewhat to do to appease and atone them, until death parted the competition and left the place to Leicester, who was not long alone without his rival in grace and command. And to conclude this favorite, it is confidently affirmed that lying in his last sickness he gave this caveat to his friends: "I am now passing into another world, and I must now leave you to your fortunes and to the Queen's grace and goodness, but beware of the gypsy," meaning Leicester, "or he will be too hard for you all. You know not the beast so well as I do."

3. Cecil: Senior

I come now to the next which was Secretary William Cecil,[63] for on the death of the old Marquess of Winchester, he came up in his room.[64] A person of most subtle and active spirit, who although he stood not altogether by way of contestation and making up of a party and faction (for he was wholly intentive to the service of Her Majesty), yet his dexterity, experience, and merit challenged a room in the Queen's favor which eclipsed the other's[65] overseem-

WILLIAM CECIL, LORD BURGHLEY

ing greatness and made it appear that there were others that steered and stood at the helm beside himself, and more stars in the firmament of her grace besides *ursa major,* or the bear with the ragged staff.

He was born (as they say) in Lincolnshire but (as some upon knowledge aver) of the younger brother[66] of the Cecils of Herefordshire, a family of my own knowledge, though now private yet of no mean antiquity, who being exposed and sent to the city, as poor gentlemen use to do their sons, became to be a rich man on London bridge[67] and purchased in Lincolnshire, where this man was born. He was sent to Cambridge and then to the Inns of

Court, and so came to serve the Duke of Somersetshire in the time of his Protectorship as secretary, and having a pregnancy to great inclinations, he came by degrees to a higher conversation with chiefest affairs of state and council. But on the fall of the Duke he stood some years in umbrage and without employment, till the estate found and needed his abilities. Although we find that he was not taken into any place during Queen Mary's reign, unless (as some have said) towards the last,[68] yet the council at several times made use of him, and in the Queen's entrance he was admitted Secretary of Estate. Afterwards he was made Master of the Court of Wards, then Lord Treasurer.

A person of most exquisite abilities, and indeed the Queen began then to need men of both garbs. And so I conclude and rank this great instrument of state amongst the *togati,* for he had not to do with the sword more than as the great paymaster[69] and contriver of the war which shortly followed, wherein he accomplished much through his own rhetorical[70] knowledge at home and his intelligence abroad by unlocking of the councils of the Queen's enemies.

We must take it[71] and that of truth into observation that until the tenth of the Queen's reign, her times were more calm and serene though sometimes a little overcast as the most glorious sunrisings are subject to shadowings and droppings, for the clouds of Spain and vapors of the Holy League[72] began to disperse and threaten her felicity.

Moreover, she was then to provide for intestine storms which began to gather in the very heart of the kingdom, all which had relation and correspondency with the other to disenthrone her and to disturb the public tranquillity and therewithal as a principal mark the established religion. For the name of recusant began then and first to be known to the world. Until then Catholics were no more than church papists, but now commanded by the Pope's express letters to appeal and forbear churchgoing as they tendered their holy father and the Roman Catholic church their mother, so then it seems the Pope had then his aims to take a true muster of his children. But the Queen had the greater advantage, for she likewise then took tale of her apostate subjects, their strength and how many there were that had given up their names to Baal,[73] who then by the hands of some of his proselytes fixed his bulls on the gates of Paul's, which discharged her subjects from all fidelity and laid seige to the received faith and so under the veil of the next successor to replant the Catholic religion. So that the Queen had then a new task and work in hand that might well awake her best providence and required a muster of men of arms as well as courtships and councils, for the time then began to grow quick and active, fitter for stronger motions than for carpet and measure.

And it will be a true note of magnanimity that she loved a soldier and had a propension in her nature to regard and always to grace them, which falling into the courtiers' consideration, they took as an invitation to win honor together with their mistress' favor by exposing themselves in the wars, especially when the Queen and the affairs of the kingdom stood in some necessity of the soldier. For we have many instances of the sallies of the nobility and gentry, yea, and of the court and of her prime favorites that had any touch or tincture of Mars in their inclinations and to steal away without license and the Queen's privity, which had like to have cost some of them dear, so predominant were their thoughts and hopes of honor grown in them as we may truly observe in the expeditions of Sir Philip Sidney, my Lord of Essex, Mountjoy, and diverse others, whose absence and their many eruptions were very distasteful unto her. Whereof I can add a true and pertinent story and that of the last Mountjoy, who having twice or thrice stolen away into Britanny (where under Sir John Norris he had then a company) without the Queen's leave or privity, she sent a messenger to him with a strict charge to the general to see him sent home. When he came into the Queen's presence, she fell into a kind of reviling, demanding how he durst go over without her leave. "Serve me so," quoth she, "once more and I will lay you fast enough for running. You will never leave till you are knocked on the head as that inconsiderate fellow Sidney was. You shall go when I send you. In the meantime see that you lodge in the court," which was then at Whitehall, "where you may follow your book, read, and discourse of wars."

But to our purpose. It fell out happily to those and (as I may say) to these times, that the Queen during the calm of her reign was not idle nor rocked asleep with security, for she had been very provident in the reparation and augmentation of her shipping and munition. And I know not whether by a foresight of policy or any instinct it came about or whether it was an act of her compassion, but it is most certain she sent levies and no small troops to the revolted states of Holland before she received any affront from the King of Spain that might seem to tend to a breach or hostility, which the papists to this day maintain was provocation of the after wars. But omitting what might be said to this point, these Netherland wars were the Queen's seminaries and nurseries of many brave soldiers, and so were likewise the civil wars of France, whither she sent five several armies, the fence schools that inured the youth and gallantry of the kingdom, and it was a militia wherein they were daily acquainted with the discipline of the Spaniards, who were then turned the Queen's inveterate enemies.

And thus have I taken into observation her *dies Halcionii,* those years of hers which were more serene and quiet than those that followed, which though they were not less propitious as being touched more with the point of honor and victory yet were they troubled and overclouded ever both with domestic and foreign machinations, and (as it is already quoted) they were such as awakened her spirits and made her cast about her to defend rather by offending,[74] and by way of diversion to prevent all invasions than to expect them, which was a piece of the cunning of the times. And with this I have noted the causes and *principia* of wars following and likewise pointed to the seed plot from whence she took up those brave men and plants of honor which acted on the theater of Mars and on whom she dispersed the rays of her grace, which were persons in their kinds of rare virtues and such as might out of right of merit pretend interest to her favor, in which rank the number will equal if not exceed that of the *togati.* In recount of whom I proceed with Sir Philip Sidney.

4. Sidney

He was the son of Henry Sidney, Lord Deputy of Ireland and president of Wales, a person of great parts and of no mean grace with the Queen.[75] His mother was sister to my Lord of Leicester, from whence we may conjecture how the father stood up in the place of honor and employment, so that his descent was apparently noble on both sides. And for his education, it was such as travel

SIR PHILIP SIDNEY

and the university could afford and his tutors infuse, for after an incredible proficiency in all the species of learning, he left the academical life for that of the court, whither he came by his uncle's invitation, famed beforehand by a noble report of his accomplishment. By which together with the state of his person, framed by a natural propension to arms, he soon attracted the good opinion of all men and was so highly prized in the esteem of the Queen that she thought the court deficient without him. And whereas through the fame of his desert he was in election for the kingdom of Pole,[76] she refused to further his preferment, not out of emulation of his advancement but out of fear to lose the jewel of her time.

He married the daughter, and sole heir, of Sir Francis Walsingham, the Secretary of State, a lady destined to the bed of honor, who after his deplorable death (at Zutphen in the Low Countries, where he was governor of Flushing and at the time of his uncle Leicester's being there) was remarried to my Lord of Essex and since his death to my Lord of St. Albans,[77] all persons of the sword and otherwise of great honor and virtue.

They have a very quaint and facetious figment of him that Mars and Mercury fell at variance whose servant he should be, and there is an epigrammatist that saith that Art and Nature had spent their excellencies in his fashioning, and fearing they could not end what they began, they bestowed him on Fortune, and Nature stood mute and amazed to behold her own work. But these are the petulancies of poets. Certain it is, he was a noble and matchless gentleman, and it may be justly said of him without the hyperboles of fiction, as it was of Cato Uticensis, that he seemed to be born only to that which he went about. *Versatilis ingenii,* as Plutarch hath it.[78] But to speak more of him were to make him less.

5. Walsingham

Francis Walsingham[79] (as we have said) had the honor to be Sir Philip Sidney's father-in-law. He was a gentleman, at first of a good house and of a better education, and from the university traveled for the rest of his learning. He was doubtless the only linguist of the times but knew best how to use his own tongue, whereby he came to be employed in the chiefest affairs of state. He was sent ambassador into France and stayed there leaguer long[80] in the heat of the civil wars and at the same time that Monsieur was here a suitor to the Queen.[81] And (if I be not mistaken) he played the very same part there as since Gondomar did here.[82] At his return he was taken in principal Secretary of State and for one of the great engines thereof and of the times, high in his mistress the Queen's favor and a watchful servant over her safety. They note him to have had certain curiosities and secret ways of intelligence above the rest.

But I must confess I am to seek wherefore he suffered Parry to play so long as he did on the hook before he hoist him up.[83] I have

SIR FRANCIS WALSINGHAM

been a little curious in the search thereof though I have not to do
with *arcana regalia imperii*,[84] for to know is sometimes a burden,
and I remember it was Ovid's *crimen aut error* that he saw too
much.[85] But I hope these are collaterals and of no danger. But that
Parry having an intent to kill the Queen made the way of his access
by betraying of others and impeaching the priests of his own correspondency and thereby had access and conference with the Queen
as oftentimes private and familiar discourse with Walsingham will
not be the quaere of the mystery,[86] for the Secretary might have had
ends of discovery on a further maturity of treason. But that after
the Queen knew Parry's intent, why she should then admit him to

private discourse and Walsingham to suffer him (considering the condition of assassins) and to permit him to go where and whither he listed and only under the security of a dark sentinel set over him was a piece of reach and hazard beyond my apprehension.

I must again profess that I have read many of his letters (for they were common) sent to my Lord of Leicester and of Burghley out of France, containing many fine passages and secrets, yet if I might have been beholding to his ciphers (whereof they are full) they would have told pretty tales of the times.

But I must now close him up and rank him among the *togati,* yet chief of those that laid the foundations[87] of the French and Dutch wars which was[88] another piece of his fineness and of the times, with one observation more: that he was one of the great allies of the austerian embracements,[89] for both himself and Stafford that preceded him[90] might well have been compared to the fiend in the Gospel that sowed his tares in the night, so did they seeds of division in the dark.[91]

And it is a likely report they father on him that the Queen speaking[92] unto him with some sensibility of the Spanish designs in France, "Madame," saith he, "I beseech you to be content and fear not. The Spaniard hath a great appetite and an excellent digestion, but I have fitted him with a bone[93] for these twenty years that Your Majesty shall have no cause to doubt him, provided that if the fire chance to slake which I have kindled, you will be ruled by me and now and then cast in some of your English fuel, which will revive the flame."

6. Willoughby

My Lord Willoughby[94] was one of the Queen's first swordmen. He was one of the ancient extract of the Berties but more ennobled by his mother, who was Duchess of Suffolk. He was a great master of the art military and was sent general into France and commanded the second army of five that the Queen had sent thither in aid of the French.

I have heard it spoken that had he not slighted the court he might have enjoyed a plentiful portion of her grace,[95] and it was his saying (and it did him no good) that he was none of the *reptilia,* intimating that he could not creep and crouch. Neither was the court his element, for indeed as he was a great soldier, so was he of a suitable magnanimity and could not brook the obsequiousness and assiduity of the court. And as he was then somewhat descending from youth, happily he had *animam revertendi*[96] and to make a safe retreat.

7. Bacon

And now I come to another of the *togati*, Sir Nicholas Bacon,[97] an archpiece of wit and wisdom. He was a man of law and a gentleman. He had great knowledge in the law whereby, together with his after part of learning and dexterity, he was promoted to be Keeper of the Great Seal. And being of kin to the Treasurer Burghley[98] had also the help of his hand to bring him into the Queen's great favor. For he was abundantly facetious which took much with the Queen when it suited with the season as he was well able to judge of his times. He had a very quaint saying and he used it oftentimes to very good purpose that he loved the jest well but not the loss of his friend. He would say that though he knew that *unusquisque suae fortunae faber*[99] was a true and good principle yet the most in number were those that marred themselves, but I will never forgive that man that loseth himself to be rid of his jest.

He was father to that refined wit that since hath acted a disastrous part on the public stage and of late sat in his father's room as Lord Chancellor. Those that lived in his age and from whence I have taken this little model of him give him a lively character, and they decipher him to be another Solon and the Sinon of those times, such an one as Oedipus was in dissolving of riddles.

Doubtless he was an able instrument, and it was his commendation that his head was the maul (for it was a very great one) and therein he kept the wedge that entered the knotty pieces that came to the table.

8. Knollys

Lords

9. Norris

And now I must fall back to smooth and plane a way to the rest, that is behind but not from my purpose.

There were about this time two rivals in the Queen's favor, old Sir Francis Knollys,[100] Controller of the House, and Sir Henry Norris,[101] whom she had called up at Parliament to sit with the peers in the higher house as Lord Norris of Rycote, who had married the daughter and heir of the old Lord Williams of Thame, a noble person and to whom the Queen in her adversity had been committed to safe custody and from him had received more than ordinary observances. Now such was the goodness of the Queen's nature that she neither forgot the good turns received from the Lord Williams, neither was she unmindful of this Lord Norris, whose father in her father's time and in the business of her mother died in a noble cause and in justification of her innocency.[102]

My Lord Norris had by this lady an ample issue which the Queen highly respected, for he had six sons, and all martial and brave men.[103] The first was William, his eldest, father to the late Earl of Barshire, second, Sir John Norris, vulgarly styled General Norris, third, Sir Edward Norris, Sir Thomas, Sir Henry, Sir Maximilian, men of an haughty courage and of great experience in the conduct of military affairs, and to speak in the character of their merit, they were persons of such renown and worth as future times must out of duty owe them the debt of an honorable memory.

Sir Francis Knollys was somewhat of the Queen's affinity[104] and had likewise a competent issue, for he had also William, his eldest son[105] and since Earl of Banbury, Sir Thomas, Sir Robert, and Sir Francis (if I be not a little mistaken in their names and marshaling), and there was also Lady Lettice, a sister of those, who was first Countess of Essex and after of Leicester; and these were also brave men in their times and places, but they were of the court and carpet and not led by the genius of the camp.

Between these two families there was (as it falleth out amongst great ones and competitors of favor) no great correspondency. And there were some seeds either of emulation or distrust cast between them, which had they not been disjoined in the residence of their persons (as it was the fortune of their employments, the one attending the court and the other the pavilion) surely they would have broken out into some kind of hostility, or at least they would have entwined one in the other like trees circled with ivy, for there was a time that both these fraternities met at court when there passed a challenge between them at certain exercises, the Queen and the old men being the spectators, which ended in a flat quarrel amongst them all. And I am persuaded (though I ought not to judge) that there were some relics of this feud which were (long after) the causes of the one family's extirpation almost utterly and of the other's improsperity, for it was a known truth that so long as my Lord of Leicester lived (who was the main pillar on the one side as having married the sister), none on the other side took any deep rooting in the court though otherwise they made their way to honor by their swords. And that which is of more note (considering my Lord of Leicester's use of men of arms, being afterwards sent governor to the revolted states and no soldier himself) is[106] that he made no more account of Sir John Norris, a soldier then deservedly famous and trained from a page under the discipline of the greatest captain in Christendom, the Admiral Châtillon,[107] and of command in the French and Dutch wars almost twenty years. And it is of further observation that my Lord of Essex, after Leicester deceased, though initiated to arms and honored by the General in the Portugal expedition, whether out of instigation (as it hath been thought) or out of ambition and jealousy to be eclipsed and overshadowed by the fame and splendor of this great commander, never loved him in sincerity. Moreover, and certain it is that he not only crushed and upon all occasions quelled the growth of this brave man and his famous brethren, but therewith drew on his own fatal end by undertaking the Irish action in a time when he left the court empty of friends and full fraught with his professed enemies.

But I forbear to extend myself in any further relation upon this subject as having left some notes of truth in these two noble families which I would present, and therewith touched somewhat which I would not if the equity of the narration would have admitted an omission.

10. Perrot

Sir John Perrot[108] was a goodly gentleman and of the sword, and of a very ancient descent as an heir to many subtracts of gentry, especially from Guy de Bryan of Lawhern,[109] so was he of a vast estate and came not to the court for want. And to these advancements he had the endowment of courage and height of spirit, had he lighted on the alloy and temper of discretion. The defect thereof, with a native freedom and boldness of speech, drew him on to a clouded setting,[110] and laid him upon the spleen and advantage of his enemies, amongst whom Sir Christopher Hatton was professed. He was yet a wise man and a brave courtier but rough, consisting more of active than sedentary motions, as being by his constellations destined for arms.

There is a quaere of some denotation how he came to receive the foil and that in the catastrophe, for he was strengthened with honorable alliances and the prime friendships of the court, my Lord of Leicester and Burghley were both his contemporaries and familiars, but that there might be (as the adage hath it) falsity in friendship, and we may rest satisfied that there is no dispute against fate. And they quote him for a person that loved to stand too much alone and on his own legs, and of too often recesses and discontinuance from the Queen's presence, a fault which is incompatible with the ways of the court and favor.

He was sent Lord Deputy into Ireland as it was then apprehended for a kind of haughtiness of spirit and repugnancy in counsels, or (as others have thought) as the fittest person then to bridle the insolency of the Irish. And probable it is that both these (considering the sway he would have at the board and had in the Queen's favor) concurred and did alike conspire his remove and ruin. But into Ireland he went, where he did the Queen many great and good services, if the surplusage of the measure did not abate the value of the merit, as aftertimes found that to be no paradox. For to save the Queen's purse, which both himself and the Lord Treasurer Burghley ever took for good service, he imposed on the

Irish the charge of bearing their own arms,[111] which both gave them the possession and taught them the use of weapons, which proved in the end a most fatal work, both to the profusion of blood and treasure.

But at his return and at some account sent home before touching the state of the kingdom, the Queen poured out assiduous testimonies of her grace towards him, till by his retreat to his castle of Cary (where he was then building) and out of a desire to be in command at home as he had been abroad, together with the hatred and practice of Hatton,[112] then in high favor, whom he had not long before too bitterly taunted for his dancing, he was accused of high treason, and for high words and a forged letter condemned, though the Queen on the news of his condemnation swore by her wonted oath that the jury were all knaves. And they deliver it with assurance that at his return to the Tower after his trial, he said, with oaths and fury, to the Lieutenant Sir Owen Hopton, "What, will the Queen suffer her brother to be offered up as a sacrifice to the envy of my strutting adversaries?"

Which being made known to the Queen and the warrant for his execution tendered and somewhat enforced, she refused to sign it and swore he should not die for he was an honest and faithful man. And surely though not altogether to set up our faith and rest upon tradition and old report as that Sir Thomas Perrot his father was a Gentleman to the Privy Chamber to Henry the Eighth and in the court married to a lady of great honor and of the King's familiarity, which are presumptions to some men, but if we go a little further and compare his picture, his qualities, his gesture and voice with that of the King's, which memory yet retains amongst us, they will plead strongly that he was a surreptitious child of the blood royal. Certain it is that he lived not long in the Tower, and that after his decease Sir Thomas Perrot his son,[113] then of no[114] mean esteem with the Queen, having before married my Lord of Essex his sister since Countess of Northumberland, had restitution of his lands, though after his death also (which immediately followed) the crown reassumed the estate and took advantage of the former attainder. And to say the truth, the priest's forged letter was at his arraignment thought but as a fiction of envy and was soon after exploded by the priest's confession.[115]

But that which most exasperated[116] the Queen and gave advantage to his enemies was (as Sir Walter Ralegh takes into his observation)[117] words of disdain, for the Queen by sharp and reprehensive letters had nettled him, and thereupon sending[118] others of approbation commending his service and intimating an invasion from Spain, which he no sooner perused but he said publicly in the great chamber at Dublin, "Lo, now she is ready to bepiss herself for fear of the Spaniard, I am again one of her white boys." Words which are subject to a various construction and tending to some disreputation of his sovereign and such as may serve for instructions to persons in place of honor and command to beware of the violences of nature and especially the exorbitancies of the tongue. And so I conclude him with this double observation:

The one of innocency of his intentions, exempt and clear from the guilt of treason and disloyalty.

The other of the greatness of his heart, for at his arraignment he was so little dejected with what might be alleged and proved against him that he grew troubled with choler, and in a kind of exasperation he despised his jury, though of the order of knighthood and of the especial gentry, claiming the privilege of trial by the peers and baronage of the realm, so prevalent was that of his native genius and haughtiness of his spirit which accompanied him to his last and till (without any diminution of courage) it broke in pieces the cords of his magnanimity, for he died suddenly in the Tower and when it was thought the Queen did intend his enlargement with the restitution of his possessions, which were then great and comparable to most of the nobility.

11. Hatton

Sir Christopher Hatton[119] came to the court (as his opposite Sir John Perrot was wont to say) by the galliard, for he came thither as a private gentleman of the Inns of Court in a masque, and for his activity and person (which was tall and proportionable) taken into the Queen's favor. He was first made vice-chamberlain and shortly after advanced to the place of Lord Chancellor.

A gentleman that beside the graces of his person and dancing had also the additament of a strong and subtle capacity, one that could soon learn the discipline and garb both of the times and court. And the truth is he had a large proportion both of gifts and endowment but too much of the season of envy, and he was a mere vegetable of the court that sprung at night and sunk again at his noon.

12. Nottingham

My Lord of Effingham[120] though a courtier betimes yet I find not that the sunshine of her favor broke out upon him until she took him into the ship and made him High Admiral of England. For his extract, it might suffice that he was the son of a Howard and of a Duke of Norfolk.

And for his person as goodly a gentleman as the times had any, if nature had not been more intentive to complete his person than fortune to make him rich. For the time considered, which was then active and a long time after lucrative, he died not rich and wealthy yet the honester man, though it seems the Queen's purpose was to tender the occasion of his advancement and to make him capable of more honor. At his return from the Cádiz voyage and action, she conferred it upon him, creating him Earl of Nottingham to the great discontent of his colleague my Lord of Essex, who then grew excessive in the appetite of her favor and (the truth is) so exorbitant in the limitation of the sovereign aspect that it much alienated the Queen's grace from him and drew others together with the Admiral to a combination and to conspire his ruin. And though (as I have heard it from that party, I mean of the Admiral's faction) that it lay not in his power to hurt my Lord Essex, yet he had more fellows and such as were well skilled in setting the gins. But I leave this to those of another age.

It is out of doubt that the Admiral was a brave, honest, and good man and a faithful servant to his mistress, and such an one as the Queen out of her own princely judgment knew to be a fit instrument for her service, for she was a proficient in the reading of men as well as books, and his sundry expeditions (as that aforementioned and eighty-eight) do both express his worth and manifest the Queen's trust and the opinion she had of his fidelity and conduct.

Moreover, the Howards were of the Queen's alliance and consanguinity by her mother, which swayed her affection and bent it towards this great house, and it was a part of her natural propension to grace and support ancient nobility where it did neither entrench nor invade her interest, for on such trespasses she was quick and tender, and would not spare any whatsoever, as we may observe in the case of the Duke[121] and my Lord of Hertford,[122] whom she much favored and countenanced till they attempted the forbidden fruit, the fault of the last being in the severest interpretation but a trespass of encroachment, but in the first it was taken for a riot against the crown and her own sovereign power, and (as I have ever thought) the cause of her aversion from the rest of that house and the Duke's great father-in-law Fitzalan, Earl of Arundel,[123] a person in the first rank of her affections before these and some other jealousies made a separation between them. This noble lord and Lord Thomas Howard[124] (since Earl of Suffolk) standing alone in her grace, the rest in her umbrage.

13. Pakington

Sir John Pakington[125] was a gentleman of no mean family, and of form and feature no ways disabled; for he was a brave gentleman and a very fine courtier, and for the time he tarried there (which was not lasting) very high in her grace. But he came in, and went out, and through disassiduity drew the curtain between the light of her grace and himself, and then death overwhelms the remnant and utterly deprives him of recovery. And they say of him that had he brought less to the court, he might have carried away more than he brought; for he had a fine time of it, but he was an ill husband of opportunity.

14. Hunsdon

My Lord of Hunsdon[126] was of the Queen's nearest kindred, and on the decease of Sussex both he and his son[127] successively took the place of the Lord Chamberlain. He was a fast man to his prince and firm to his friends and servants, and though he might speak big and therein would be borne out, yet was he not the more dreadful but less harmful and far from the practice of my Lord of Leicester's

HENRY CAREY, LORD HUNSDON

instructions, for he was downright. And I have heard those that both knew him well and had interest in him say merrily of him that his Latin and dissimilation were both alike and that his custom of swearing and obscenity in speaking made him seem a worse Christian than he was and a better knight of the carpet than he could be. As he lived in a ruffling time so he loved sword and buckler men, and such as our fathers were wont to call men of their hands, of which sort he had many brave gentlemen that followed him yet not taken for a popular and dangerous person.

And this is one that stood amongst the *togati*, of an honest and stout heart and such an one as upon occasion would have fought for his prince and country, for he had the charge of the Queen's person both in the court and also in the camp at Tilbury in eighty-eight.

15. Ralegh

Sir Walter Ralegh[128] was one that it seems fortune had picked out of purpose of whom to make an example or to use as her tennis ball thereby to show what she could do, for she tossed him up of nothing, and to and fro, and from thence down to little more than that wherein she found him, a bare gentleman; not that he was less,

SIR WALTER RALEGH

for he was well descended and of good alliance, but poor in his beginnings. And as for my Lord of Oxford's jest of him, for a jack and an upstart, we all know it savored more of emulation and his humor than the truth.[129]

And it is a certain note of the times that the Queen in her choice never took into her favor a mere new man or a mechanic, as Comines observes[130] of Louis the Eleventh, who did serve himself with persons of unknown parents, such as were Oliver the barber, whom he created Earl of Dunois and made his *ex secretis conciliis* and alone in his favor and familiarity.

His approaches to the university and Inns of Court were the grounds of his improvement, but they were rather excursions than sieges or sitting down, for he stayed not long in a place, and being the youngest brother and the house diminished in its patrimony, he foresaw his own destiny that he was first to roll through want and disability to subsist before he could come to a repose and as the stone doth by lying long gather moss. He first exposed himself into the land service of Ireland,[131] a militia, which did not then yield him food and raiment for it was ever poor. Nor had he patience to stay long there though shortly after he came thither again under the command of my Lord Grey[132] but with his colors flying in the field, having in the interim cast a new chance both in the Low Countries and in a voyage to the sea. And if ever man drew virtue out of necessity, it was he, and therein was he the great example of industry, and though he might then have taken that of the merchant to himself, *Per mare per terras currit mercator ad Indos*,[133] he might also have said and truly with the philosopher, *Omnia mea mecum porto*,[134] for it was a long time before he could brag of more than he carried at his back. And when he got on the winning side it was his commendation that he took pains for it and underwent many various adventures for his after perfection and before he came to the public note of the world. And that it may appear how he came up *per ardua, per varios casus, per tot discrimina rerum*,[135] not pulled up by chance nor by any gentle admittance of fortune, I will briefly describe his native parts and those of his own acquiring which were the hopes of his rising.

He had in the outward man a good presence in a handsome and well-compact person, a strong wit naturally and a better judgment, with a bold and plausible tongue whereby he could set out his part to the best advantage, and to these he had the adjunct of some general learning which by diligence he enforced to a great augmentation and perfection, for he was an indefatigable reader whether by sea or land and none of the least observers both of the men and the times. And I am somewhat confident that amongst the second causes of his growth, that variance between him and my Lord General Grey[136] in his second voyage into Ireland was a principal one, for it drew them both over to the Council table, there to plead their own cause. Where what advantage he had in the case in controversy I know not, but he had much the better in the manner of telling his tale, insomuch that the Queen and the lords took no slight notice of him and his parts, for from thence he came to be known and to have access to the Queen and the lords, and then we are not to doubt how such a man could comply and learn the way to progression. And whether or no my Lord of Leicester had then cast in for him a good word to the Queen (which would have done him no harm) I do not determine, but true it is he had gotten the Queen's ear in a trice and she began to be taken with his elocution and loved to hear his reasons to her demands.

And truth it is she took him for a kind of oracle, which nettled them all; yea, those that he relied on began to take this sudden favor for an alarm and to be sensible of their own supplantation and to project his, which made him shortly after to sing, "Fortune my foe, etc."[137] So that finding his favor declining and falling into a recess, he undertook a new peregrination, to leave the *terra infirma* of the court for that of the waves and by declining himself and by absence to expel his and the passion of his enemies, which in court was a strange device of recovery. But that he then knew there was some ill office done him, yet he durst not attempt to amend it by any other way than by going aside, thereby to teach envy a new way of forgetfulness and not so much as to think of him. Howsoever, he had it always in mind never to forget himself. And his device took so well that at his return he came in (as rams do by going backward) with greater strength and so continued till her last, great in her grace and captain of her guard. Where I must leave him but with this observation, that though he gained much at the court, yet he took it not out of the exchequer or merely of the Queen's purse but by his wit and by the help of the prerogative, for the Queen was never profuse in delivering out of her treasure but paid many and most of her servants part in money and the rest in grace, which as the case then stood was good payment, leaving the arrear of recompense due to their merit to her great successor, who paid them all with advantage.[138]

16. Greville

Sir Fulke Greville,[139] since Lord Brooke, had no mean place in her favor; neither did he hold it for any short time or term, for if I be not deceived, he had the longest lease and the smoothest time without rubs of any of her favorites. He came to the court in his youth and prime as that is the time or never.

He was a brave gentleman and honorably descended from Willoughby, Lord Brooke and Admiral to Henry the Seventh. Neither illiterate, for he was (as he would often profess) a friend to Sir Philip Sidney, and there are of his own extant some fragments of his pen and of the times which do interest him to the muses and which shows the Queen's election had ever a noble conduct and its motions more of virtue and judgment than of fancy.

I find that he neither sought for nor obtained any great place or preferment in court during all the time of his attendance, neither did he need it for he came thither backed with a plentiful fortune, which (as himself was wont to say) was the better held together by a single life, wherein he lived and died a constant courtier and of the ladies.

17. Essex

My Lord of Essex[140] (as Sir Henry Wotton, a gentleman of great parts and partly of his time and retinue, observes)[141] had his introduction by my Lord of Leicester, who had married his mother: a tie of affinity which beside a more urgent obligation might have invited his care to advance him, his fortunes being then and through his father's infelicity grown low. But that a son of a Lord Ferrers of Chartley, Viscount Hereford, and Earl of Essex,[142] who was of the ancient nobility and formerly of the Queen's good grace, could not have room in her favor without the assistance of

Leicester was beyond the rule of her nature, which as I have else-where taken into observation was ever inclinable to favor the no-bility. Sure it is that he no sooner appeared in court but he took with the Queen and courtiers. And I believe they all could not choose but look through the sacrifice of the father[143] on his living son whose image by the remembrance of former passages was afresh (like bleeding of men murdered) represented to the court and offered up as a subject of compassion to all the kingdom.

There was in this young lord, together with a most goodly person, a kind of urbanity, or innate courtesy, which both won the Queen and too much took upon the people to gaze on the new adopted son of her favor.

And as I go along it will not be amiss to take into observation two notable quotations. The first is a violent indulgence of the Queen, which is incident to old age where it encounters with a pleasant and suitable object, towards this great lord and which argued a nonperpetuity. The second was a fault in the object of her grace, my lord himself, who drew in fast[144] like a child sucking a uberous breast.

And had there been a more decent decorum observed in both or either of these, without doubt the unity of their affections had been more permanent and not so in and out as they were, like an instrument ill tuned and lapsed to discord. The greater error of the two (though unwillingly) I am constrained to impose on my Lord of Essex, or rather on his youth, and none of the least of the blame on those that stood sentinels about him who might have advised him better, but like men intoxicated with hopes they likewise had sucked in with the most of their lord's receipt and so like Caesars would have all or none, a rule quite contrary to nature and the most indulgent parents who though they may express more love to one in the abundance of bequests, yet cannot forget some legacies and just distributives and dividends to other of their begetting. And how hateful partiality is and proves, every day's experience tells us, out of which common consideration might have framed to their hands a maxim of more discretion for the conduct and man-agement of their new graced lord and master.

But to omit that of infusion and to do right to truth, my Lord of Essex, even of those that truly loved and honored him, was noted for too bold an ingressor both of fame and favor. And of this (without offense to the living or treading on the sacred urn of the dead) I shall present a truth and a passage yet in memory.

My Lord of Mountjoy (who was another child of her favor), being newly come to court and then but Sir Charles Blount (for my Lord William, his eldest brother, was then living), had the good fortune one day to run well at tilt, and the Queen was therewith so well pleased that she sent him in token of her favor a queen at chess of gold richly enameled, which his servants had the next day fastened on his arm with a crimson ribbon, which my Lord of Essex, as he passed through the privy chamber espying, with his cloak cast under his arm the better to commend it to the view, required what it was and for what cause there fixed. Sir Fulke Greville told him it was the Queen's favor which the day before and after the tilting she had sent him. Whereat my Lord of Essex in a kind of emulation and as though he would have limited her favor said, "I perceive every fool must have a favor." This bitter and public affront came to Sir Charles Blount's ear, who sent him the challenge, which was accepted by my Lord of Essex, and they met near Marylebone Park, where my lord was hurt in the thigh and disarmed. The Queen missing the men was very curious to learn the truth, and when at last it was whispered out, she swore by God's death that some one or other should take him down and teach him better manners, otherwise there will be no rule with him. And here I note the inition of my lord's friendship with Mountjoy, which the Queen herself did then conjure.

Now for fame we need not go far, for my Lord of Essex having borne a grudge to General Norris, who had and unwittingly offered to undertake the action to Brittany with fewer men than my lord had before demanded. On his return with victory and a glorious report of his valor, he was then thought the only man for the Irish wars. Wherein my lord so wrought by despising the rebels, their number and quality, that Norris was sent over with a scanted force joined with the relics of the veteran troops of Brittany of set purpose and (as it fell out) to ruin Norris. And the Lord Borough by my lord's procurement sent at his heels and to command in chief and to confine Norris only to his government at Munster, which broke the great heart of the general to see himself undervalued and undermined by my lord and Borough, which was (as the proverb speaks it), *Imberbes docere senes.*[145]

Now my Lord Borough in the beginning of his prosecution died, whereupon the Queen was fully bent to send over my Lord Mountjoy, which Essex utterly disliked and opposed and by arguments of contempt against him[146] (his then professed friend and familiar), so predominant was his desire to reap the whole honor of closing up that war and all others. Now the way being opened and planed by his own workmanship, and so handled that none durst appear to stand for the place, at last and with much ado he obtained his own ends and therewith his fatal destruction, leaving the Queen and the court, where he stood impregnable in her grace, to men that long had watched their times to give him the trip and could never find opportunity but this of his absence and of his own creation.

And these are the true observations of his appetite and inclination, which were not of any true proportion but hurried and transported with an over desire and thirstiness after fame, and that deceitful fame of popularity. And to help on his catastrophe I observe likewise two sorts of people that had a hand in his fall.

The first was the soldiery, which all flocked unto him, as it were foretelling a mortality, and are commonly of blunt and too rough counsels and are many times dissonant from the tune of the court and state.

The other sort was of his family, his servants, and his own creatures, which were bound by the rules of safety and obligation of fidelity to have looked better to the steering of the boat wherein they themselves were carried and not to have suffered it to fleet and run aground with those empty sails of tumor of popularity and applause. Methinks one honest man or other that had but the office of brushing his clothes might have whispered in his ear, "My Lord look to it, this multitude that follows you will either devour you or undo you. Strive not to rule and overrule all, for it will cost hot water and it will procure envy, and if needs your genius must have it so, let the court and the Queen's presence be your station, for your absence will undo you."

But (as I have said) they had sucked too much of their lord's milk, and instead of withdrawing they blew the coals of his ambition and infused into him too much of the spirit of glory. Yea, and mixed the goodness of his nature with a touch of revenge, which is ever accompanied with a destiny of the same fate. Of this number there were some of insufferable natures about him that towards his last gave desperate advice, such as his integrity abhorred and his fidelity forbade, among whom Sir Henry Wotton notes[147] (without injury) his secretary Cuff as a vile man and of a perverse nature. I could also note others that when he was in the right course of recovery, setting to moderation, would not suffer a recess in him but stirred the dregs of those rude humors which, by time and his affliction out of his own judgment, he thought to depose and to give them all a vomit.

And thus I conclude this noble lord as a mixture between prosperity and adversity, once the child of his great mistress' favor, but the son of Bellona.

18. Buckhurst

My Lord Buckhurst[148] was of the noble house of the Sackvilles and of the Queen's consanguinity. His father was Sir Richard Sackville, or as the people then called him, Fillsack, by reason of his great wealth and the vast patrimony which he left to his son, whereof he spent in his youth the best part until the Queen by her frequent admonitions diverted the torrent of his profusion.[149]

He was a very fine gentleman of person and endowments both of art and nature but without measure magnificent till upon the turn of his humor and the allay that his age and good counsel had wrought upon these immoderate courses of his youth and that height of spirit inherent to his house. And then did the Queen, as a most judicious prince, when she saw the man grow settled and staid, give him her assistance and advance him to the treasurership, where he made amends to his house for his misspent time, both in the increment of his estate and honor which the Queen conferred upon him together with the opportunity to remake himself and thereby to show that this was a child that should have a share in her grace and a taste of her bounty. They much commend his elocution but more the excellency of his pen, for he was a scholar and a person of a quick dispatch, faculties that yet run in the blood. And they say of him that his secretaries did little for him by way of inditement wherein they could seldom please him, he was so facete and choice in his phrases and style. And for his dispatches and the contents he gave to suitors, he had a decorum seldom since put in practice. For he had of his attendants that took in a roll the names of all suitors with the date of their first address, and these in their order had hearing, so that a fresh man could not leap over his head that was of a more ancient edition except in the urgent affairs of the state.

I find not that he was any ways ensnared in the factions of the court, which were all his time strong and in every man's note: the Howards and the Cecils on the one part, my Lord of Essex on the other. For he held the staff of the treasury fast in his hands, which once in the year made them all beholding to him. And the truth is, as he was a wise man and a stout, he had no reason to be a partaker, for he stood fully in blood and in grace and was wholly intentive to the Queen's service, and such were his abilities that she received assiduous proofs of his sufficiency. And it hath been thought she might have had more cunning instruments but none of a more strong judgment and confidence in his ways which are symptoms of magnanimity, whereunto methinks his motto hath some kind of reference, *Aut nunquam tentes aut perfice*,[150] as though he would have charactered in a word the genius of his house or express somewhat of a higher inclination than lay in his compass. That he was a courtier is apparent, for he stood always in her eye and favor.

19. Mountjoy

My Lord Mountjoy[151] was of the ancient nobility but utterly decayed in the support thereof through his grandfather's excess in the action of Boleyn, his father's vanity in the search of the philosopher's stone, and his brother's untimely prodigalities, all which seemed by a joint conspiracy to ruinate the house and altogether to annihilate it.[152]

As he came from Oxford, he took the Inner Temple in the way to court, whither he no sooner came but had a pretty strange kind of admission which I have heard from a discreet man of his own and much more of the secrets of those times.

He was then much about twenty years, of a brown hair, a sweet face, and a most neat composure in his person. The Queen was then at Whitehall and at dinner, whither he came to see the fashion of the court. The Queen had soon found him out and with a kind of affected frown asked the Lady Carver what he was. She answered she knew him not, insomuch as inquire was made one from another who he might be till at length it was told the Queen that he was brother to the Lord William Mountjoy. This inquisition with the eye of majesty fixed upon him as she was wont to do and to daunt men she knew not stirred the blood of this young gentleman insomuch as his color came and went, which the Queen observing, she called him and gave him her hand to kiss, encouraging him with gracious words and new looks, and so diverting her speech to the lords and ladies, she said that she no sooner saw him but she knew there was in him some noble blood with some other expressions of pity towards his house. And then again demanding his name she said, "Fail you not to come to the court, and I will bethink myself how to do you good."

And this was his inlet and the beginning of his grace. Where it falls into consideration that though he wanted not wit and courage, for he had very fine attractives as being a good piece of a scholar, yet were these accompanied with the retractives of bashfulness and a natural modesty which (as the wane of the house and the ebb of his fortunes then stood) might have hindered his progression had they not been enforced by this infusion of sovereign favor and the Queen's gracious invitation.

And that it might appear how low he was and how much that heretic necessity will work in dejected souls and good spirits, I can deliver it with assurance that his exhibition was very scant until his brother died, which was shortly after his admission to the court, and then was it no more but a thousand marks per annum, wherewith he lived plentifully and in a fine garb and without any great sustentation of the Queen during all her time.

And as there was in his nature a kind of backwardness which did not befriend him nor suit with the motion of the court, so there was in him an inclination to arms with an humor of traveling and gadding abroad which had not some wise man about him labored to remove and the Queen herself laid in her commands, he would out of his own native propension have marred his own market. For as he was grown by reading (whereunto he was much addicted) to the theory of a soldier so was he strongly invited by his genius to the acquaintance of the practice of the wars, which were the causes of his excursions, for he had a company in the Low Countries from whence he came over with a noble acceptance of the Queen. But somewhat restless in honorable thoughts, he exposed himself again and again, and would press the Queen with the pretenses of visiting his company so often till at length he had a flat denial. And yet he stole over with Sir John Norris into the action of Brittany (which then was a hot and active war), whom he would always call his father, honoring him alone above all men and ever bewailing his end (so contrary he was in his esteem and valuation of his great commander to that of his friend my Lord of Essex). Till at last the Queen began to take his decessions for contempt and confined his residence to the court and her own person.

And upon my Lord of Essex' fall, so confident she was in her own princely judgment and the opinion she had conceived of his worth and conduct that she would have this noble gentleman and none other to finish and bring the Irish war to a propitious end, for it was a prophetical speech of her own that it would be his fortune and his valor to cut the thread of the fatal rebellion and to bring her in peace to her grave. Wherein she was not deceived, for he achieved it but with much pains and carefulness, but not without the fears and many jealousies of the court and times wherewith the Queen's age and the malignity of her setting times were replete.

And so I come to his dear friend in court Master Secretary Cecil, whom in his long absence from court he adored as his saint and counted for his only Maecenas, both before and after his departure from court and during all the time of his command in Ireland, well knowing that it lay in his power and by a word of his mouth to make or mar him.

20. Cecil: Robert

Sir Robert Cecil,[153] since Earl of Salisbury, was the son of the Lord Burghley and the inheritor of his wisdom and, by degrees, successor of his place and fortunes, though not of his lands, for he had Sir Thomas Cecil, his elder, since created Earl of Exeter.[154]

He was first Secretary of State, then Master of the Wards, and in the last reign came to be Lord Treasurer, all which were the steps of his father's greatness and of the honor he left to the house. For his

person, he was not much beholding to nature though somewhat
for his face, which was the best part of his outside. But for his
inside, it may be said and without solecism that he was his father's
own son and a pregnant proficient in all his discipline of state.

He was a courtier from his cradle, which[155] might have made him
betimes, yet he was at the age of twenty and upwards and was far
short of his after proof, but exposed and by change of climate he
soon made show what he was and would be.

He lived in those times wherein the Queen had most need and
use of men of weight,[156] and amongst many able ones he was a chief
as having taken his sufficiency from his instructions which begot
him and the tutorship of the times and court, which were then the
academies of art and cunning, for such was the Queen's condition
from the tenth or twelfth of her reign that she had the happiness to
stand up (whereof there is a former intimation) though environed
with many and more enemies and assaulted with more dangerous
practices than any princess of her times and many ages before.

Neither must we in this her preservation attribute too much to
human policies, for that God in his omnipotent providence had
not only ordained those secondary means as instruments of the
work but, by an evident manifestation that[157] the same work which
she acted was a well pleasing work of his own, out of a peculiar
care had[158] decreed the protection of this work-mistress and thereupon added his wonted blessing upon all and whatsoever she
undertook. Which is an observation of satisfaction to myself that
she was in the right, though to others now breathing under the
same form and frame of government it may not seem an animad-
version of any worth. But I leave them to the peril of their own
folly.

And so again to this great master of state and the staff of the
Queen's declining age, who though his little crooked person could
not promise any great supportation yet it carried thereon a head
and a headpiece of a vast content. And therein it seems nature was
so diligent to complete one and the best part about him, as that to
the perfection of his memory and intellectuals, she took care also
of his senses and to put him *Lynceus* eyes,[159] or to pleasure him the
more, borrowed of Argus so to give him a perspective sight. And
for the rest of the sensitive virtues, his predecessor Walsingham
had left him a receipt to smell out what was done in the conclave
and his good old father was so well seen in the mathematics that he

could tell you throughout all Spain every part, every port, every ship with their burdens, whither bound, what preparation, what impediments for diversion of enterprises, counsels, and resolutions.

And that we may see as in a little map how docile this man was, I will present a taste of his abilities. My Lord of Devonshire[160] upon the certainty that the Spaniard would invade Ireland with a strong army had written very earnestly to the Queen and the Council for such supplies to be timely sent over that might enable him to march both up to the Spaniard if he did land and follow on his prosecution without[161] diverting his intentions against the rebels. Sir Robert Cecil, besides the general dispatch of the Council, as he often did wrote thus in private, for those two began to love dearly:

My Lord: Out of the abundance of my affection and the care I have of your welldoing, I must in private put you out of doubt (for I know you cannot be sensible otherwise than in the way of honor) that the Spaniard will not come upon you this year, for I have it from my own what his preparations are in all parts and what he can do, for be confident he beareth up a reputation by seeming to embrace more than he can grip. But the next year, be sure, he will cast over unto you some forlorn troops, which how they may be reinforced beyond his present ability and first intention I cannot as yet make any certain judgment. But I believe, out of my intelligence, that you may expect their landing in Munster and (the more to distract you) in several places, as at Kinsale,[162] Beerhaven, and Baltimore, where you may be sure (coming from sea) they will first fortify and learn the strength of the rebels before they dare take the field. Howsoever (as I know you will not) lessen not your care, neither your defenses, and whatsoever lies in my power to do you and the public good service rest thereof assured.[163]

And to this I could add much more, but it may (as it is) suffice to present thus much as his abilities in the pen, that he was his craftsmaster in foreign intelligences and for domestic affairs. As he was one of those that sat at the stern to the last of the Queen so was he none of the least in skill and true use of the compass. And so I shall only vindicate the scandal of his death and conclude him.[164] For he departed at Saint Margaret's in his return from Bath, as my Lord Viscount Chamberlain, my Lord Clifford, myself, his son,

and son-in-law and many more can witness. But that the day
before he swooned on the way and was taken out of his litter and
was laid into his coach was a truth out of which that falsehood
concerning the manner of his death and its derivation, though
nothing to the purpose or to the prejudice of his worth.

21. Vere

Sir Francis Vere[165] was of the most ancient and of the most noble
abstract of the Earls of Oxford, and it may be a question whether
the nobility of his house or the honor of his achievements might
most commend him but that we have an authentic rule to decide
the doubt: *Et genus et proavos et quae non fecimus ipsi vix ea
nostra voco.*[166] For though he were an honorable slip of that ancient
tree of nobility, which was no disadvantage to his virtues, yet he
brought more glory to the name of Vere than he took of blood
from the family.

He was amongst all the Queen's swordsmen inferior to none but
superior to many. Of whom it may be said: To speak much of him
were the way to leave out somewhat that might add to his praise
and to forget more that would make for his honor.

I find not that he came much to the court for he lived almost
perpetually in the camp,[167] but when he did, no man had more of
the Queen's favor and no less envy, for he seldom troubled it with
the noise and alarms of supplantation; his way was another sort of
undermining.

They report of the Queen as she loved martial men yet would
court this gentleman as soon as he appeared in her presence. And
surely he was a soldier of great worth and commanded thirty years
in the service of the States and twenty years[168] over the English, in
chief as the Queen's general,[169] and he that had seen the battle at
Newport might there best have taken him and his noble brother,
my Lord of Tilbury,[170] to the life.

22. Worcester

My Lord of Worcester[171] I have here put last but not least in the
Queen's favor. He was of the ancient and noble blood of the

Beaufords and of her grandfather's line by the mother which the Queen could never forget, especially when there was an incurrence of old blood with fidelity, a mixture which ever sorted with the Queen's nature. And though there might appear somewhat in his house which might invert her grace (though not to speak of my lord himself but with due reverence and in honor), I mean contrariety and suspicion in religion,[172] yet the Queen ever respected this house and principally this noble lord, whom she first made Master of Her Horse and then admitted him to her Council of State.

In his youth (part whereof he spent before he came to reside at court) he was a very fine gentleman and the best horseman and tilter of the times, which were then the manlike and noble recreations of the court and such as took up the applause of men as well as the praise and commendation of the ladies. And when years had abated those exercises of honor, he grew then to be a most faithful and profound councillor. And as I have placed him last so was he the last liver of all the servants of her favor and had the honor to see his renowned mistress and all of them in their places of rest. And for himself, after a life of a very noble and remarkable reputation, he died rich and in a peaceable old age. A fate that I make the last and none of my slightest observations, which fell not out on many of the rest, for they expired like unto lights blown out with the snuff stinking, not commendably extinguished and without offense to the standers by.

Conclusion

And thus I have delivered up my poor essay or little draft of this great princess and her times with the servants of her state and favor. I cannot say I have finished it, for I know how defective and imperfect it is as limned only in the original nature not with active blemishes, and so left it as a task fitter for remoter times and to sallies of some bolder pencil to correct that which is amiss and to draw the rest to life. As for me to have endeavored it, I took it into consideration how easily I might have dashed in too much of the strain of pollution and thereby have defaced that little which is done. For I profess I have taken care so to master my pen that I might not *ex animo,* or of set purpose, discolor truth or any of the parts thereof otherwise than in concealment. Happily there are some which will not approve of this modesty but will censure it for pusillanimity and with cunning artists attempt to draw their line out at farther length and upon this of mine, which may with somewhat more ease be affected for that the frame is ready made to their hands, and happily I could draw one in the midst of theirs but that modesty in me forbids the defacement of men departed whose posterity yet remaining enjoys the merit of their virtues and do still live in their honor. And I had rather incur the censure of abruption than to be conscious and taken in the manner of sinning by eruption and in trampling on the graves of persons at rest which living we durst not look in the face or make our addresses to them otherwise than with due regard to their honors and reverence to their virtues.

Finis.

Laus Trinuni Deo.

Appendix
The Manuscript Copies

1. Folger MS. G. a. 11
2. Folger MS. G. b. 21
3. Folger MS. G. b. 20
4. Folger MS. G. b. 19
5. British Library, Sloane MS. 868
6. British Library, Sloane MS. 876
7. British Library, Stowe MS. 161
8. British Library, Stowe MS. 278
9. British Library, Stowe MS. 619
10. British Library, Lansdowne MS. 254
11. British Library, Lansdowne MS. 238
12. British Library, Harleian MS. 7393
13. British Library, Harleian MS. 3787
14. British Library, Harleian MS. 1704
15. British Library, Harleian MS. 6842
16. British Library, Add. MS. 5499
17. British Library, Add. MS. 22591
18. British Library, Add. MS. 28715
19. Trinity College, Dublin, MS. 1045
20. Bodleian Library, Malone MS. 20
21. Harvard University, Unnumbered MS.
22. Harvard University, Unnumbered MS.

A collation of two hundred random variants indicates the following division into groups of manuscripts containing similar readings:

A. 4, 8, 11, 14, and sometimes 6 and 15.
B. 2 and 9.

    C. 1, 12, and 22.
    D. 17 and 21.
    E. 3 and 16.
    F. 7, 10, 18, 19, 20, and sometimes 5 and 13.

   Groups D, E, and F have a tendency toward agreement. Unfortunately, there is still too great a variation among the texts of any one of the groups for the editor to determine a single manuscript (or, for that matter, any one group) as the basis for the others. This conclusion agrees, as the editor later found out, with R. B. McKerrow's observation that manuscript texts (unlike printed editions) seldom have any extant common "ancestor," but represent the end products of many different lines of descent.[1]

Notes

Chapter 1. The Life of Sir Robert Naunton

1. The essential biographical facts relating to Naunton's early life are from Sidney Lee, "Naunton, Sir Robert," in the *Dictionary of National Biography*. All information is found there unless otherwise noted.
2. Cambridge University, *The Book of Matriculations and Degrees . . . from 1544 to 1659*, ed. John Venn and J. A. Venn (Cambridge, 1913), 481.
3. Naunton's contribution:

In obitum nobilissimi clarissimiq̃; Herois
D. Philippi Sydneij equitis aurati.

Cvi Dea nascenti praesto lucina manebat,
Cui nato admôrunt charites, atque ubera Musae,
Cui sua magnus *Apollo* dedit, sua *Iuno, Venusq̃,*
Symbola certatim dederant; huic munere perdit.
Dum geminata parat, geminato munere perdit.
Quippe ut utroq̃; suum *Sydneium* illustret honore,
Vult Musis Martem, vult aegida iungat olivae,
Omnia dum dare vult, rapid heû rapit omnia habentem.

4. *Calendar of State Papers relating to Scotland, 1547–1603,* 13 vols. (Edinburgh and Glasgow, 1898–1969), 9:596, 620.
5. Ibid., 10:130.
6. Ibid., 116, 118.
7. Ibid., 218, 239.
8. Ibid., 24.
9. Ibid., 116–17.
10. Cambridge University, *Alumni Cantabrigienses,* ed. John Venn and J. A. Venn, 10 vols. (Cambridge, 1922–54), 1:44.
11. *Scot. Cal.,* 10:119.
12. "The summary of the cause in the case of Robert Naunton vs. Robert Chester," Huntington Library, MS. EL-6058.
13. *Calendar of State Papers, Domestic Series . . . 1547–1625,* 12 vols. (London, 1856–72), addenda, 221.
14. Thomas Birch, *Memoirs of the Reign of Queen Elizabeth,* 2 vols. (London, 1754), 1:399.
15. Ibid., 368.

16. William Camden, *History of the Most Renowned and Victorious Princess Elizabeth, Late Queen of England,* 3d ed., rev. (London, 1675), 485. See also Gregorio Marañon, *Antonio Pérez,* trans. Charles Ley (London, 1954), 312–15.

17. Birch, *Reign of Queen Elizabeth,* 1:435–36.

18. Huntington Library, MS. EL-6058; Birch, *Reign of Queen Elizabeth,* 1:466.

19. Birch, *Reign of Queen Elizabeth,* 2:7. The phrase "be a seaman" refers to the Cádiz expedition that left England a few weeks later.

20. Ibid., 210.

21. Ibid., 212–13.

22. Ibid., 286.

23. Ibid., 304.

24. Ibid., 367–69.

25. Huntington Library MS. EL-6058; MS. EL-6056, "The answer of Robert Chester in the case of Robert Naunton vs. Robert Chester."

26. *Alumni Cantabrigienses,* s.v. "Chester, Robert" and "Tuckfield, Henry."

27. Huntington Library, MSS. EL-6055–EL-6058, *Four Manuscripts concerning the case of Robert Naunton vs. Robert Chester.*

28. *Cal. S.P. Dom., 1601–3,* addenda, 221.

29. Historical Manuscripts Commission, *Salisbury,* 12:124; 13:233.

30. Quoted in Dorothea Coke, *The Last Elizabethan: Sir John Coke, 1563–1644* (London, 1937), 7.

31. Howell says that "at the beginning of his Speech, when he had pronounced *Serenissime Rex,* he was dashed out of countenance, and so gravelled [i.e., confused] that he could go no further" (James Howell, *Epistolae Ho-Elianae,* ed. Joseph Jacobs, 2 vols. [London, 1892], 1:294).

32. James Whitelocke, *Liber Famelicus,* ed. John Bruce (Westminster, 1858), 29.

33. *The Letters of John Chamberlain,* ed. Norman E. McClure, 2 vols. (Philadelphia, 1939), 1:526, 529.

34. William A. Shaw, *The Knights of England,* 2 vols. (London, 1906), 2:156.

35. For the family relationship between Naunton and Villiers see James Jermyn, *A Stemma of the Naunton Family,* British Library Add. MS. 17098 (1806).

36. Chamberlain, *Letters,* 2:30.

37. *Cal. S. P. Dom., 1611–18,* 492.

38. Chamberlain, *Letters,* 2:128–29.

39. Hist. MSS Com., *Coke,* 1:95–96.

40. Florence May Evans, *The Principal Secretary of State: A Survey of the Office from 1558 to 1680* (Manchester, 1923), 73–4.

41. *Cal. S. P. Dom., 1619–23,* 15.

42. Arthur Wilson, *The History of Great Britain, Being the Life and Reign of King James the First* (London, 1653), 97.

43. Chamberlain, *Letters,* 2:161.

44. *The Letters and the Life of Francis Bacon,* ed. James Spedding, 7 vols. (London, 1861–74), 6:320.

45. *Cal. S. P. Dom., 1611–18,* 565.

46. See A. F. Pollard, "Wilson, Sir Thomas," in *Dictionary of National Biography.*

47. *Cal. S. P. Dom., 1611–18,* 570, 574–75, 583.

48. *A Declaration of the Demeanor and Carriage of Sir Walter Ralegh,* reprinted in *Harleian Miscellany,* 10 vols. (London, 1808–13), 3:32.

49. *Fortesque Papers,* ed. S. R. Gardiner (Westminster, 1871), 57.

50. *Harleian Miscellany,* 3:32.

51. Chamberlain, *Letters,* 2:185.

52. *Fortesque Papers,* 67.

53. Chamberlain, *Letters,* 2:188.

54. *The History of the Worthies of England,* ed. John Nichols, 2 vols. (London, 1811), 2:336. Mr. Wiemark made his witticism in December 1618 (see *Cal. S. P. Dom., 1611–18,* 601). The meeting for the contributions for St. Paul's was not until April 1620 (Chamberlain, *Letters,* 2:301).

55. For a detailed analysis of the business handled by the Secretary at this time and the limited power of decision allowed him, see Evans, *Principal Secretary of State,* 75–77. Much of Naunton's official correspondence is included in *Cal. S. P. Dom., 1619–23.*

56. For Naunton's correspondence dealing with this matter, see *Letters and Other Documents Illustrating the Relations between England and Germany at the Commencement of the Thirty Years' War,* ed. S. R. Gardiner (Westminister, 1865), *passim; The Autobiography of Edward, Lord Herbert, of Cherbury,* ed. Sidney L. Lee (London, 1886), 339–48.

57. *Cal. S. P. Dom., 1619–23,* 199, 203.

58. *Calendar of State Papers and Manuscripts relating to English Affairs, Existing in the Archives and Collections of Venice, and in Other Libraries of Northern Italy,* 38 vols. (London, 1864–1947), 1617–19, 565.

59. Hist. MSS Com., *Coke,* 1:110.

60. Chamberlain, *Letters,* 2:272, 251.

61. British Library, Harleian MS. 1581, quoted in John Nichols, *The History and Antiquities of the County of Leicester,* 4 vols. (London, 1795–1815), 3:516.

62. Chamberlain, *Letters,* 2:266, 316.

63. *Ven. Cal., 1619–21,* 402.

64. Chamberlain, *Letters,* 2:318.

65. *Ven. Cal., 1619–21,* 432.

66. *Members of Parliament,* 4 vols. (London, 1878–91), 1:450.

67. *Cal. S. P. Dom., 1619–23,* 215.

68. *Ven. Cal., 1619–21,* 534–35.

69. Chamberlain, *Letters,* 2:336.

70. *Ven. Cal., 1621–23,* 68.

71. Chamberlain, *Letters,* 2:395.

72. *Cal. S. P. Dom., 1619–23,* 293, 481; see also *Ven. Cal., 1621–23,* 108; Chamberlain, *Letters,* 2:399.

73. Nichols, *History and Antiquities of Leicester,* 3:516.

74. Chamberlain, *Letters,* 2:470.

75. Ibid., 474.

76. *Ven. Cal., 1623–25,* 9.

77. *Members of Parliament,* 1:456.

78. *Cal. S. P. Dom., 1623–25,* 148.

79. Chamberlain, *Letters,* 2:568.

80. *Cal. S. P. Dom., 1623–25,* 319.

81. Ibid., 346.

82. Nichols, *History and Antiquities of Leicester,* 3:518 (misnumbered *514).

83. *Ven. Cal., 1625–26,* 4.

84. *Members of Parliament,* 1:462, 471.

85. See *Cal. S. P. Dom., 1628–29,* 326; ibid., 1631–33, 60; Hist. MSS Com.,

Coke, 2:22.
86. Hist. MSS Com., *Coke,* 2:60.
87. *The Earl of Strafford's Letters and Dispatches,* ed. William Knowler, 2 vols. (London, 1740), 1:412.
88. Hist. MSS Com., *Coke,* 2:64.
89. *Strafford's Letters and Dispatches,* 1:372, 389, 412.

Chapter 2. Naunton's Work

1. Hist. MSS Com., *Coke,* 2:22; *Strafford's Letters and Dispatches,* 1:369.
2. See *Fragmenta Regalia,* 42, 67.
3. See ibid., 46–47.
4. Although this work was not published until 1641, manuscript copies had been in circulation much earlier (see Logan Pearsall Smith, *The Life and Letters of Sir Henry Wotton,* 2 vols. [Oxford, 1907], 2:206).
5. See *Fragmenta Regalia,* 57, 82.
6. The passages from Camden are recorded below in the notes to the *Fragmenta Regalia.*
7. In the sketch of Hunsdon. And although the date at this point is omitted in many copies of the work and may be a scribal addition, it also appears in the sketch of Charles Howard, first Earl of Nottingham.
8. This form is the subject of D. Nichol Smith's introduction to his collection, *Characters from the Histories and Memoirs of the Seventeenth Century* (Oxford, 1918).
9. *Collected Works,* eds. J. Spedding, R. L. Ellis, and D. D. Heath, 14 vols. (London, 1857–74), 6:291.
10. Edited by Evelyn Plummer Read and Conyers Read (Philadelphia, 1951).

Chapter 3. The Text of the *Fragmenta Regalia*

1. In the absence of any evidence to the contrary, I have accepted the order of the two 1641 editions given by Donald Wing in his *Short-Title Catalogue of Books . . . 1641–1700* (New York, 1945–51). 1641(A) is W. 249 and 1641(B) is W. 250. Neither edition was entered in the *Stationer's Register.*
2. Henry R. Plomer, "Eliot's Court Press, Decorative Blocks and Initials," *Library,* 4th ser., 3:199. The head ornament is reproduced in plate 9.
3. Listed by Plomer in "The Eliot's Court Printing House, 1584–1674," *Library,* 4th ser., 2:175.
4. Ronald B. McKerrow, *A Dictionary of Printers and Booksellers in England, Scotland and Ireland, and of Foreign Printers of English Books, 1557–1640* (London, 1910), 6. The device is also reproduced in idem, "Edward Allde as a Typical Trade Printer," *Library,* 4th ser., 10:121, plate 19.
5. Henry R. Plomer, *A Dictionary of the Booksellers and Printers Who Were at Work in England, Scotland, and Ireland from 1641 to 1667* (London, 1907), 142. Plomer says that Oulton was the son of Elizabeth Allde by her first husband. However, the account in McKerrow states that Ralph Joyner was her first husband and that her son by him was also named Ralph.

6. An example of this is the printing of *joy* (page 22, line 27, 1642 edition) instead of *ivy.* This was the result of misreading the spelling *yvie* found in some of the manuscript copies (including Folger MS. G. a. 11).

7. For the principal variations in all five editions, see John S. Cerovski, *Sir Robert Naunton's FRAGMENTA REGALIA or Observations on Queene Elizabeth Her Times & Favourites, A Critical Edition* (Ann Arbor, Mich.: University Microfilms, 1961).

8. *Arcana Aulica; or, Walsingham's Manual . . . To which is added Fragmenta Regalia; or, Observations on Queen Elizabeth, Her Times, and Favorites* (London, 1694), Sigs, A7ᵛ–A8ᵛ.

9. For a list of these and the relationships among them, see Appendix.

10. The entries in the Thorpe catalogs do not give any information regarding the manuscript's previous history.

Chapter 4. *Fragmenta Regalia*

1. bed] G. b. 21; blood G. a. 11. This reading has the support of all the early editions and all but a few of the manuscripts. "Austria" obviously should be "Aragon." However, all the manuscripts and printed editions examined read "Austria," so the error seems to be a lapse by Naunton or, possibly, a scribal error that occurred early in the text's history.

2. This and the following paragraph are an expansion of William Camden, *Annales Rerum Anglicarum et Hibernicarum Regnante Elizabetha* (London, 1615–27), 1. As translated by Norton, the passage reads: "The lineage and descent of Elizabeth, Queen of England, was by her father's side truly royal, for daughter she was to King Henry the Eighth, granddaughter to Henry the Seventh, and great-granddaughter to Edward the Fourth. By the mother's side her descent was not so high, howbeit noble it was and spread abroad by many and great alliances throughout England and Ireland" (William Camden, *The History of the Most Renowned and Victorious Princess Elizabeth, Late Queen of England,* trans. R. Norton [London, 1630], sig. B4).

3. Sir Geoffrey Boleyn, a wealthy London merchant, Lord Mayor in 1457. He was the great-grandfather of Anne.

4. "For building an ancient house."

5. accumulation] G. b. 21; Emulation G. a. 11.

6. bond,] G. b. 21; boone, and G. a. 11.

7. Naunton's description of the young Queen is based either on contemporary accounts or pictures (such as the so-called Ermine Portrait, ascribed to Nicholas Hilliard, at Hatfield House). In the 1590s, when Naunton probably saw Elizabeth, she was described by the German traveler Paul Hentzner as having an oblong face, "fair but wrinkled; her eyes small, yet black and pleasant; her nose a little hooked; her lips narrow, and her teeth black" (*Paul Hentzner's Travels in England during the Reign of Queen Elizabeth,* trans. Horace [Walpole], late Earl of Orford [London, 1797], 34).

8. I.e., the execution of Mary Stuart, Queen of Scots (see John Bennett Black, *The Reign of Elizabeth, 1558–1603* [Oxford, 1936], 332–35).

9. From Ps. 118:23, "This is the Lord's doing; it is marvelous in our eyes"; and Ps. 18:2, "My God, my strength, in whom I will trust."

10. "Sharers of care."

11. Piers Gaveston, Earl of Cornwall (d. 1312), favorite of Edward II, used his great influence unwisely. He figures as one of the major characters in Marlowe's *Edward II.* Robert de Vere, ninth Earl of Oxford and Duke of Ireland (1362–92), was a favorite of Richard II. Hugh le Despenser, the elder, Earl of Winchester (1262–1326), and his son Hugh le Despenser, the younger (d. 1326), who after Gaveston's death took his place as favorites of Edward II, used their influence to further their own interests.

12. I.e., a prime favorite.

13. The principal figures of the opposing factions in Elizabeth's court were Burghley (standing for the moderate course of action, the Anglicans, and the commercial class) and Leicester (standing for the Puritans, the fighting men, and the militants). Walsingham, Warwick, Knollys, and Bedford were on Leicester's side; Sussex sided with Burghley. The same factions continued later in the reign with Essex on one side and Robert Cecil on the other (see Alfred L. Rowse, *The England of Elizabeth* [New York, 1951], 281–83; Conyers Read, "Factions in the English Privy Council under Elizabeth," American Historical Association, *Annual Report for 1911,* 1 : 113–19).

14. "Mr. Bowyer, the Gentleman Usher" is referred to by Mary Sidney in a letter to Edward Mollineux in 1578 (Arthur Collins, ed., *Letters and Memorials of State . . . Written and Collected by Sir Henry Sidney . . . Sir Philip Sidney and His Brother Sir Robert Sidney . . .,* 2 vols. [London, 1746], 1 : 272). Possibly he was Robert Bowyer, who was later a secretary to Thomas Sackville and sat in the House of Commons (see *The Parliamentary Diary of Robert Bowyer, 1606–1607,* ed. D. H. Willson [Minneapolis, Minn., 1931], ix).

15. I.e., not to be meddled with (see Gen. 49 : 16–17).

16. "Touch me not" (see John 20 : 17).

17. though] G. b. 20; thought G. a. 11.

18. Naunton is probably referring to Hugh O'Neill, the second Earl of Tyrone (1540?–1616), and his negotiations with the court.

19. I.e., grants of land by charter.

20. In *The History of the World* (London, 1614), 1(5) : 717–18.

21. their] G. b. 21; her G. a. 11.

22. to] G. b. 20; *omit* G. a. 11.

23. alarm] alarme G. b. 21; watch Alay G. a. 11.

24. the state and] G. b. 21; and the state of G. a. 11.

25. According to one account, 400,000 pounds (see Bowyer, *Parliamentary Diary,* 43).

26. Richard Martin (1570–1618), Recorder of London, celebrated as a wit. Jonson dedicated his *Poetaster* to him.

27. The story referred to is found in Valerius Maximus, *Facta et Dicta Memorabilia,* 8.14.5. However, Naunton probably has in mind a speech made to the Parliament by King James in 1604 in which he complains about the Commons and uses the same story (see D. Harris Willson, *King James VI and I* [London, 1956], 249).

28. I.e., Charles I.

29. ignorant] G. b. 21; to learn G. a. 11.

30. Richard Carmarden, "perhaps the best informed and most reliable of Queen Elizabeth's customs officials" (J.U. Nef, quoted by Rowse in *England of Elizabeth,* 114). Carmarden is particularly noted for his vigorous action on behalf of the Queen's interest. In 1595 he caused several ships belonging to the London merchant Leveson to be impounded for abuses of the customs (George B. Harri-

son, *A Second Elizabethan Journal* [New York, 1931], 45). His name is variantly spelled *Carmarden, Carmarthen,* and *Carwarden* in the *Fragmenta* manuscripts and in other contemporary documents.

31. Thomas Smythe (d. 1591), a haberdasher who made a fortune from operating the customs of the port of London by lease from the government. For the period 1584–88, he paid a large rental fee of 30,000 pounds and yet made a profit of 16,000 pounds (Rowse, *England of Elizabeth,* 331).

32. This story of Carwarden is also found in Ralegh, *The Prerogative of Parliaments in England* (Middelburg, 1628), 39, and in Camden, *Annales* (1627), 4:20–21.

33. The impositions were duties levied by the King without parliamentary authority in order to augment his revenues. The King's right to levy the impositions was hotly contested in the Parliament of 1610 (see Godfrey Davies, *The Early Stuarts, 1603–1660* [Oxford, 1937], 10–13).

34. Edward I had required landowners having property worth twenty pounds a year to be knighted. Acting on this precedent, Charles I, in January 1630, called on all freeholders of forty pounds or more to pay for knighthood. In this way the crown raised 115,000 pounds by October 1631 (F. C. Montague, *The History of England, 1603–1660* [London, 1907], 168).

35. She retained eleven of Mary's councillors and added seven new ones of her own choice (Conyers Read, *The Tudors* [New York, 1936], 147).

36. gists] G. b. 21; gifts G. a. 11. The stopping places in a monarch's travels.

37. Sir Francis Englefield (d. 1596), a staunch Catholic, had held positions of high rank under Queen Mary. He fled England because, as he said, his conscience "was not made of wax." He was attainted, and through dubious proceedings the crown confiscated his manor and estates, which had been in his family for more than 780 years.

38. William Paulet, first Marquess of Winchester (1485?–1572). His first court appointment was as Master of the Court of Wards under Henry VIII in 1526. Other positions with their accompanying rewards followed. As Naunton says, he continued in the service of the court through the succeeding reigns. The preacher John Knox spoke out against him in a sermon in 1553 and in doing so referred to his "counsel and wit," which, along with his pliability, seem to have been his sustaining qualities. Anne Boleyn did not include him in her complaints against Henry's council. In a letter to Burghley in 1560, he wrote that "worldly things would sometimes fall out contrary, but if quietly taken could be quietly amended." He was a great favorite of Elizabeth and remained active at the court in spite of his extreme age until his death in 1572 (see also Rowse, *England of Elizabeth,* 324–25).

39. William Herbert, first Earl of Pembroke (1501?–70), was made a gentleman pensioner and esquire to the body of Henry VIII in 1526, the same year that Paulet entered court service. Like Paulet he remained long in favor and was rewarded accordingly. He was one of Henry VIII's executors, a member of Edward VI's council, president of Wales in 1550, governor of Calais in 1556, and a captain-general in the army. He nearly came to grief for joining Northumberland in proclaiming Lady Jane Grey on 10 July 1553, but declared for Mary within a week's time and retained his position at court.

40. Henry Herbert married Lady Catherine Grey in May 1553 at the instigation of John Dudley, Duke of Northumberland. The union was never consummated and under the influence of Queen Mary (not Elizabeth, as implied in Naunton's account) was dissolved. Henry was married to Katherine, daughter of

George Talbot, Earl of Shrewsbury, from 1563 until her death in 1575. The marriage with Mary Sidney did not take place until 1577.

41. Robert Dudley, Baron Denbigh, Earl of Leicester (1532?–88). He was knighted in Edward VI's reign. As Naunton says, he was Elizabeth's first favorite. He was made Master of the Horse in 1558 and soon afterward a member of the Privy Council; suspected of having brought about the death of his wife, Amy, 1560; created Baron of Denbigh and Earl of Leicester, 1564; secretly married Lady Sheffield, 1573, whose husband he was said to have poisoned; took part in Drake's expedition, 1577; married Lettice Knollys, Countess of Essex, 1578; commanded an expedition to assist the United Provinces against Spain, 1585, and was chosen governor, 1586; carried on an indecisive campaign against the Spaniards and was recalled, 1587. He died of a fever, or, according to some, of poison, in 1588.

(The brief introduction to each of the characters is intended to supply the reference of dates that is lacking in Naunton's text. Unless otherwise noted, the information is from *The Dictionary of National Biography*.)

42. Sir John Dudley, Viscount Lisle, Earl of Warwick, Duke of Northumberland (1502?–53). He was beheaded for proclaiming his daughter-in-law, Lady Jane Grey, queen and actively supporting her rather than Mary Tudor.

43. Edmund Dudley (1462?–1510) and Richard Empson (d. 1510) were associated under Henry VII in the collection of taxes and feudal dues. They were accused of using overrigorous methods in fulfilling their duty. Francis Bacon, in his biography of Henry, charges them with going far beyond the law:

> These two persons being lawyers in science and privy counsellors in authority (as the corruption of the best things is the worst) turned law and justice into wormwood and rapine. For first their manner was to cause diverse subjects to be indicted of sundry crimes and so far forth to proceed in form of law; but when the bills were found, then presently to commit them, and nevertheless not to produce them in any reasonable time to their answer but to suffer them to languish in prison, and by sundry artificial devices and terrors to extort from them great fines and ransoms, which they termed compositions and mitigations. (*Works*, 6:325)

Bacon accuses them not only of extortion but also of the sale of pardons and offices. They were executed at the beginning of Henry VIII's reign in response to public demand.

44. I.e., Northumberland, John Dudley.

45. I.e., to seize or take by violence or extortion; to plunder, as by excessive taxation.

46. He had called for his armed followers as a protection for the time of the death of Henry VII. The order was construed as a treason plotted against the new King.

47. and fuel] G. b. 21; of fewell G. a. 11.

48. Epilepsy, but used facetiously to refer to a fall from power or favor.

49. Edward Seymour, first Earl of Hertford, and Duke of Somerset (1506?–52). He was beheaded after serving as Protector of the Crown during the reign of Edward VI.

50. I.e., the Protector's (Edward Seymour) and his brother Thomas's.

51. Ambrose Dudley (1528?–90). He inherited the estate since he was the older of the two. He was created Earl of Warwick in 1561.

52. Johnson defines *aftergame* as "the scheme which may be laid or the expedients which are practiced after the original game has miscarried." Naunton seems to mean that Leicester depended more on immediate action and first opinions than on careful consideration, i.e., "after wit." Something of such an attitude is contained in John Clapham's description of Leicester as "being very hardly reconciled where he had once conceived offense" (Clapham, *Elizabeth of England*, 91).

53. I.e., backward or ill prepared.

54. The reference is to Robert Cecil, Earl of Salisbury.

55. election] G. b. 21; affection G. a. 11. Cf. the following passage from Clapham:

> She had in her time four principal favorites: namely, the Earl of Leicester, Sir Christopher Hatton, Sir Walter Raleigh, and the Earl of Essex. All these successively enjoyed her grace in the highest measure, being men of very comely personage, and adorned with all outward gifts of nature, but much differing one from another in the disposition of their minds. (*Elizabeth of England*, 90)

56. By Ben Jonson, for one, in his *Conversations with William Drummond of Hawthornden:* "The Earl of Leicester gave a bottle of liquor to his lady, which he willed her to use in any faintness, which she, after his return from court, not knowing it was poison, gave him, and so he died" (ed. R. F. Patterson [London, 1923], 31).

57. The most notorious of these was "The copy of a letter written by a Master of Art of Cambridge to his friend in London concerning some talk past of late between two worshipful and grave men about the present state and some proceedings of the Earl of Leicester and his friends in England," popularly known as "Leicester's Commonwealth." It was the work of an anonymous courtier who described Leicester as being a professional poisoner and a debauchee. It was first printed in 1584; French and Latin translations were printed in the following year.

58. Walter Devereux, first Earl of Essex, and second Viscount Hereford (1541?–76). After his death a report was prevalent that Leicester had poisoned him. His "lady" was Lettice Knollys, the Countess of Essex, whom Leicester married in 1578. After Leicester's death she married Christopher Blount in 1589. She died at the age of ninety-four in 1634. She was, therefore, still alive at the time of Naunton's writing.

59. Rowse suggests a somewhat different interpretation: "He [Leicester] spoke and read Italian; he was splendid and mean; he carried himself like a Renaissance prince" (*England of Elizabeth*, 282).

60. "I came, I saw, I went back."

61. Sussex] Thomas Radcliffe, third Earl of Sussex (1526?–83). He was appointed Lord Deputy of Ireland under Queen Mary in 1556 and put down a rebellion headed by Shane O'Neill. Elizabeth reappointed him to the same position, which he held until 1564. As Lord President of the North he put down the rebellion of 1569 and pursued the rebels, Dacre and Westmorland, into Scotland. He was admitted to the Privy Council in 1570 and was made Lord Chamberlain in 1572. The antagonism between Sussex and Leicester seems to have been the result of Leicester's criticism of Sussex's conduct in Ireland. Sussex strongly opposed the proposal that Leicester should become Elizabeth's husband and supported the negotiations for a foreign match.

62. friends] G. b. 21; friend G. a. 11.

63. William Cecil, Lord Burghley (1520–98), the son of Richard Cecil, a squire

in the service of Henry VIII. He was educated at Cambridge, 1535–41, and at Gray's Inn, 1541. His first official position was as Master of Requests, 1547. He was made personal secretary to Lord Protector Somerset, 1548; Secretary of State, under Warwick, 1550; knighted 1551. Under Queen Elizabeth, he was Secretary of State, 1558–72; Master of the Court of Wards, 1561; created Baron Burghley, 1571; succeeded Winchester as Lord High Treasurer, 1572. The Queen designated Burghley as holding the first place in her realm in 1565, and his position never became less.

64. I.e., as Lord High Treasurer.

65. I.e., Leicester's. The bear with the ragged staff was the insignia of the Dudley family.

66. brother] G. b. 21; brothers G. a. 11.

67. There is no evidence to support this statement, either with reference to David Cecil, who settled at Stamford in Lincolnshire, or the Richard Cecil, William's father, who was born there (see Conyers Read, *Mr Secretary Cecil and Queen Elizabeth* [London, 1955], 17–22).

68. Actually not. Early in the reign of Mary he acted as a diplomatic escort for Cardinal Pole and sat in Parliament. During the last three years of Mary's reign he was inactive (Read, *Cecil*, 102–6).

69. His concern for the pay of the common soldier is particularly remembered in the anonymous contemporary biography printed in Francis Peck, ed., *Desiderata Curiosa*, 2 vols. in 1 (London, 1732–35), 1:38.

70. rhetorical] Theoricall G. b. 21.

71. For this and the following paragraph, cf. Camden, *Annales* (1615), 271–72:

Till this time a fair calm weather shone upon the papists in England, who through a certain merciful connivance had their own service of God in their private houses in a manner without punishment, although it were prohibited by the law, a pecuniary mulct being inflicted. Neither did the Queen think that their consciences were to be forced. But after such time as that thunderbolt of excommunication was shot forth at Rome against the Queen, this fair weather vanished by little and little into clouds and tempests, and drew forth a law in the year 1571 against those should bring into the realm such bulls, agnus deis, and blessed grains, privy tokens of papal obedience, or should reconcile any man to the church of Rome. (Trans. Norton [1630], 2:86–87)

72. Holy League] G. b. 20; holy-land G. a. 11. As explained by Camden: "The popish princes of France, with the privity of the bishop of Rome and the Spaniard, secretly entered into a most dangerous conspiracy, under color of defending the catholic religion, by the name of the Holy Union or League" (Trans. Norton [1630], 4:11).

73. The reference seems to be to the canvas made in November 1569 of the justices of peace, county by county, who were called to declare their obedience to the Act of Uniformity. The canvas followed a governmental crisis involving a conspiracy instigated by the Spanish ambassador de Spes to increase the power of the Catholics in England by the marriage of Mary, Queen of Scots, to Thomas Howard, Duke of Norfolk (Read, *Cecil*, 439–53).

74. Cf. Henry Wotton, *The State of Christendom* . . . (London, 1657), 108: "Why should it be a fault imputed unto our Queen, that she relieveth her oppressed neighbors, since she doth it not in malice towards the Spaniards, but in

mercy towards the afflicted; not so much to offend him, as to defend them, not to enlarge her dominions, but to preserve her realms and subjects." Although not published until 1657, this work was written in 1594 (see L. P. Smith, *Sir Henry Wotton*, 2:455–56).

75. Sir Philip Sidney (1554–86), soldier, statesman, and poet; son of Sir Henry Sidney; educated at Shrewsbury and Oxford; traveled extensively on the Continent, 1572–75; entrusted with diplomatic missions to the Netherlands, Heidelberg, and Prague, 1577; knighted and named Master of the Horse, 1583; married Frances, daughter of Secretary Walsingham, 1583; secretly tried to join Drake's expedition, 1585; recalled to court, but made governor of Flushing; joined an attack on a Spanish convoy for the relief of Zutphen, wounded in the thigh, and died at Armhem, 1586.

76. For a repudiation of this story see Mona Wilson, *Sir Philip Sidney* (London, 1931), 319.

77. Richard de Burgh (d. 1635).

78. Cato . . . *Versatilis ingenii*] The phrase is found in Livy, 39. 40, and is used to describe Cato Major, the Censor, not Cato Uticensis (this information was included in a note by the editor of the 1824 edition of the *Fragmenta*, 68).

79. Sir Francis Walsingham (1530?–90), entered Elizabeth's diplomatic service in the decade following her accession. He was educated at Cambridge and at Gray's Inn; brought up a zealous Protestant; traveled on the Continent during Queen Mary's reign, 1553–58; member of Parliament for Banbury, 1559; collected foreign intelligence for Cecil; chief of the secret service in London, 1569; tracked out the Ridolfi plot, 1569; envoy to Paris to ask indulgence for the Huguenots, 1570; ambassador at Paris to negotiate a French alliance and Queen Elizabeth's marriage with Anjou, 1570–73; protected English Protestants during the Saint Bartholomew's Day Massacre, 1572; Secretary of State, 1573–90; knighted, 1577; secured the conviction of William Parry, 1585, of Anthony Babington, 1586, and of Mary, Queen of Scots, 1586. With the Lord High Treasurer Burghley, Walsingham was responsible for the administration of Elizabeth's government.

80. I.e., as resident ambassador in the autumn of 1570.

81. Henry, Duke of Anjou, later Henry III, King of France. It was at the "same time" (ca. 1571) that he was a suitor of the Queen, but he was not "here" (i.e., in England).

82. Count of Gondomar, Diego Sarmiento de Acuña (1567–1626). He was Spanish ambassador to England, 1613–18 and 1619–22. The part he played included protecting those of his own religion and something in the nature of spying.

83. William Parry was executed in March 1585 after being found guilty of conspiring to murder Elizabeth. Parry had been in Burghley's intelligence service on the Continent and had established contacts with the Pope and with Mary Stuart's agent in Paris, who had suggested an attempt on Elizabeth's life. After his return to England in January 1584, Parry played the part of informer to the Queen. In the following year he proposed a plot to assassinate the Queen to Edmund Neville, who reported him to the court. Parry claimed he had only been trying to draw Neville out, but the court thought differently. Camden has the following account of Parry's plot against the Queen:

This Parry . . . being returned about two years before out of Italy, had to the end to win favor and credit with the Queen, privily revealed what . . . other fugitives had treated concerning the taking away of her life by wicked hand, pretending that he had dealt with them to no other intent then to spy out their secret attempts and so provide for the Queen's safety. Hereupon she did not lightly give credit to Neville, the informer, yet commanded Walsingham to ask Parry whether he had dealt about this matter with any malcontented and suspected person, to feel him. He flatly denied it, and being otherwise a man quick-sighted enough, yet saw he not the evasion which the Queen's leniency had laid open upon him. For if he had but given any inkling that he had dealt with Neville, only to feel him, whom the Queen had already told him to be a suspected and malcontented man, he had without doubt avoided the danger. But a wicked deed once concluded doth many times dull the sharpest wits. But whereas Neville had no witness to maintain his accusation, Parry was brought to confront him, who after some biting words one against another, relented a little, and being sent to the Tower of London, confessed voluntarily these things. (Trans. Norton [1630], 3:43–44)

Of Naunton's criticism of Walsingham, Read says that Walsingham, like the Queen, probably had accepted Parry's explanation that he had been acting a double part in order to gain information, and that even if Walsingham had intercepted Parry's letters there is no reason to assume that they excited his suspicions since it was quite in keeping with the part that Parry proposed to play for him to have written such (Conyers Read, *Mr. Secretary Walsingham and the Policy of Queen Elizabeth*, 3 vols. [Oxford, 1925], 2:403).

84. "The royal secrets of empire."

85. Ovid's "crime or error" was that he witnessed a crime committed by a member of the royal household. At least this is the traditional story offered to explain Ovid's banishment by Augustus.

86. mystery] G. b. 21; misery G. a. 11.

87. By his encouragement of the Protestants (see Read, *Walsingham*, 1:261).

88. which was] G. b. 21; with G. a. 11.

89. austerian] G. b. 21; Austrian G. a. 11. I.e., Puritanism (see Read, *Walsingham*, 2:261).

90. Sir Edward Stafford (1522?–1605). He did not precede Walsingham but followed him. He carried on the negotiations for the Alençon marriage from 1578 to 1581 and was appointed resident ambassador to France in October 1583. Like Walsingham he was a zealous Protestant.

91. I.e., by their support of the Protestants in France.

92. speaking] G. b. 20; said G. a. 11.

93. I.e., the rebellion against the Spaniards in the Low Countries (see James Howell, *Epistolae Ho-Elianae*, ed. Joseph Jacobs, 2 vols. [London, 1892], 1:120).

94. Peregrine Bertie, Lord Willoughby de Eresby (1555–1601), soldier. He was the son of Richard and Catharine Bertie, who were fleeing from Marian persecution when he was born at Cleves. He was naturalized in England, 1559; succeeded to the Barony of Eresby, 1580; sent on a diplomatic mission to Denmark, 1582; governor of Bergen-op-Zoom, 1586. He served in the Netherlands campaigns from 1586 to 1589. In 1587 he succeeded Sir John Norris in command of the cavalry, and, later in the same year, the Earl of Leicester in command of the English troops. In September 1589 he was commander of an army sent to aid Henry of Navarre at Dieppe, and took part in the capture of Vendôme, Mons, Alençon, and Falaise. He returned to England in 1590. He was governor of Berwick and warden of East March, 1589–1601.

95. Willoughby, like the Queen's other poorly rewarded servants (Walsingham, for example), depleted his own estate in her service. His correspondence to the court contains numerous and continual pleas for funds and supplies to feed and clothe his troops (see Georgina Bertie, *Five Generations of a Loyal House* [London, 1845], 149, 151, *et passim*).

96. "The spirit to return."

97. Sir Nicholas Bacon (1509–79) studied common law at Gray's Inn and was called to the bar in 1533. Upon the accession of Elizabeth he was appointed Lord Keeper of the Great Seal, admitted to the Privy Council, and knighted. In 1559 he was authorized to exercise the jurisdiction of Lord Chancellor.

98. His close friendship with Burghley originated when they were both students at Cambridge. Burghley later married Mildred Cooke, a sister of Bacon's second wife.

99. *unusquisque . . . faber*] G. b. 21; *unusquisqe was fortunae faber* G. a. 11. "The mould of a man's fortune is in his own hands. *Faber quisque fortunae suae,*" as it appears in the essay "On Fortune" by Bacon's son Francis (*Works*, 6:215). Francis Bacon is the "refined wit" referred to in the following paragraph.

100. Sir Francis Knollys (1514?–96), statesman. He was educated at Oxford; attended Anne of Cleves on her arrival in England, 1539; M.P. for Horsham,1542; knighted, 1547; favored by Edward VI. A fervent Puritan, he spent the five years of Mary's reign in Germany. He was admitted a member of the Privy Council upon Elizabeth's accession and for the rest of his life was prominently active in various offices of state.

101. Henry Norris, Baron Norris of Rycote (1525?–1601), son of Henry Norris (who was executed in 1536 for a suspected intrigue with Anne Boleyn). The King later restored much of the family's estate. Norris was appointed sheriff of Oxfordshire and Berkshire, 1561; knighted and appointed ambassador to France, 1566; created Baron Norris of Rycote, 1572.

102. His execution as the alleged lover of Anne Boleyn. During his trial he pleaded both his own and Anne's innocence.

103. For this and the following paragraph, cf. Camden, *Annales* (1627), 4:256–57:

> Henry, Lord Norris of Rycote . . . begat on Margaret his wife, one of the heirs of John Lord Williams of Thame (who in the reign of Henry the Eighth was treasurer of the Court of Augmentations, and a privy counsellor to Queen Mary, who most entirely respected him), a brood of martial men, namely, William, his eldest son, marshal of Barwick, which died in Ireland (to whom was born Francis, which succeeded in his grandfather's honor); John, whom I have already often mentioned; Thomas, president of Munster, and for a little while Lord Justice of Ireland, who died of a light wound neglected; Henry, which died there the same death almost at the same time; Maximilian, which was slain in the British war; and Edward, governor of Ostend, who alone survived his parents. (Trans. Norton [1630], 4:200–201)

104. His wife, Catherine Carey, was a first cousin of Elizabeth.

105. William Knollys, Earl of Banbury (1547–1632). He was the oldest surviving son; Henry, who died about 1583, was the firstborn. In all, Knollys had seven sons and four daughters; Naunton names only the sons who lived on into the reign of King James.

106. is] G. b. 21; as G. a. 11.

107. Gaspard de Châtillon, Comte de Coligny (1519–72), Admiral of France, and Protestant leader.

108. Sir John Perrot (1527?–92), commonly thought to be a son of Henry VIII by Mary Berkley (afterward the wife of Thomas Perrot). He served as president of Munster from 1570 to 1573, and was successful in forcing the submission of the rebel James Fitzgerald. He was appointed Lord Deputy of Ireland in 1584. He returned to England in disgrace in 1588 as a result of indiscreet behavior and was committed to the Tower. He died in the Tower of London after being found guilty of high treason in 1592.

109. Sir Guy de Bryan (d. 1390), Lord High Admiral, 1370, one of the earliest K.G.'s under Edward III (see Joseph Hadyn, *The Book of Dignities* [London, 1890], 733).

110. setting] G. b. 21; sitting G. a. 11.

111. Cf. *Camden, Annales* (1615), 476:

Till this time (to digress a little) had the English men very easy wars in Ireland. . . . But after that they were by Perrot's commandment trained daily at home, taught to use their weapons, and to discharge their pieces at a mark that they might be the more ready servitors against the Hebridians, and afterwards being bred up in the Netherland wars they had learned the manner of fortifications, they then certainly exercised the English (as we shall see) with a more difficult war. (Trans. Norton [1630], 3:127)

112. The rumored reason for Hatton's antipathy for Perrot was that Perrot had seduced the illegitimate daughter of Hatton (see Eric St. John Brooks, *Sir Christopher Hatton* [London, 1946], 15, 358–59). The strongly contrasting personalities of the two men seem a sufficient reason for their dissension: Hatton, the well-mannered courtier, and Perrot, the coarse, outspoken soldier.

113. Robert Naunton's father-in-law. Naunton married Penelope, daughter of Thomas by Dorothy Devereux.

114. no] G. b. 20; *omit* G. a. 11.

115. The forgery was purported to be a letter from Perrot to Philip of Spain, promising that if Philip would give him Wales, Perrot would make Philip master of England and Ireland. Although the letter was disproved, the substance was, nevertheless, incorporated as part of the indictment against Perrot.

116. exasperated] G. b. 21; respected G. a. 11.

117. In his *History of the World*, 1(5):337.

118. sending] G. b. 21; seeing G. a. 11.

119. Sir Christopher Hatton (1540–91) was another of the courtiers constantly in the Queen's favor. He was educated at Oxford; became one of Elizabeth's gentlemen pensioners, 1564; received grants of estates, court offices, and an annuity; captain of the bodyguard, 1572; charged by Mary, Queen of Scots, with being Elizabeth's paramour, 1584; made vice-chamberlain and knighted, 1578; Lord Chancellor, 1587–91; K.G., 1588; Chancellor of Oxford, 1588.

120. Charles Howard (1536–1624), second Baron Howard of Effingham, first Earl of Nottingham, was Lord Chamberlain from 1574 to 1585. He was appointed Lord High Admiral in 1585, held chief command against the Armada, and was in charge of the sea forces of the Cádiz expedition in 1596. He was in continuous high favor with the Queen.

121. Thomas Howard, fourth Duke of Norfolk (1536–72). He was involved in the Ridolfi plot and executed for treason.

122. Sir Edward Seymour, Baron Beauchamp and Earl of Hertford (1539?–1621). Disregarding an act of 1536, which stated that it was treason to marry a person of royal blood without the consent of the crown, he secretly married Lady Catherine Grey in 1560.

123. Henry Fitzalan, twelfth Earl of Arundel (1511?–80).

124. lord, and Lord Thomas Howard] G. b. 20; Lord Thomas Howard, G. a. 11.

125. Sir John Pakington (1549–1625). His wit and beauty attracted the Queen's attention in 1575, and he was invited to the court in London, where his extravagant manner of living depleted his fortune within a few years. The Queen called him "lusty Pakington" because of his athletic abilities. Although the Queen aided him financially, it was only after his retirement to his estates in Worcestershire and a wealthy marriage that he was able to pay his debts.

126. Henry Carey, first Lord Hunsdon (1524?–96). He was active in Scottish affairs and although Naunton labels him as one of the "togati" and a "knight of the carpet," he led many of the military campaigns against the Scots. In 1583 he was made Lord Chamberlain. At the time of the Spanish Armada, Hunsdon was in charge of a force of 36,000 formed as the Queen's bodyguard at Tilbury Fort. He was of the "Queen's nearest kindred" through his mother Mary, Anne Boleyn's sister (i.e., he was first cousin to Elizabeth).

127. George Carey, second Lord Hunsdon (1547–1603), was appointed Lord Chamberlain in 1597.

128. Sir Walter Ralegh (1552?–1618), educated at Oxford; served in France in the Huguenot army, 1569; sailed to Ireland as captain of a company, 1580; knighted, 1584; obtained a patent to take possession of unknown lands in America in Queen Elizabeth's name, 1584; placed on a commission to draw up a plan of defense against the expected invasion from Spain, 1588; found his influence somewhat lessened by a quarrel with Essex, 1588; was committed to the Tower by Queen Elizabeth, who discovered that he had carried on an affair with Elizabeth Throckmorton; was released but, subsequently marrying Elizabeth Throckmorton, was forbidden the court; undertook an expedition to search for the fabled city Manoa, 1595; participated in the Cádiz expedition, 1596; the Azores expedition, 1597. He was deprived of most of his offices on the accession of James I; was sent to the Tower on the charge of conspiring against James, found guilty but was reprieved, 1603; lived in the Tower until 1616, when his friends succeeded in persuading James to permit him to undertake another expedition in search of gold; returned unsuccessful to England, 1618; his punishment demanded by the Spanish minister on the news of the expedition's destruction of San Tomás; was arrested and lodged in the Tower; executed in Old Palace Yard, Westminister, in persuance of his former (1603) sentence, on 29 October 1618.

129. The anecdote referred to is included in Bacon's *Apophthegms:*

When Queen Elizabeth had advanced Ralegh, she was one day playing on the virginals, and my Lord of Oxford and another nobleman stood by. It fell out so, that the ledge before the jacks was taken away, so as the jacks were seen. My Lord of Oxford and the other nobleman smiled, and a little whispered. The Queen marked it, and would needs know what the matter was. My Lord of Oxford answered, "That they smiled to see that when jacks went up heads went down." (*Works*, 7:124)

130. Philippe de Comines (1445–1511), in *The History of Philip de Comines*

Knight, Lord of Argenton, trans. Thomas Danett (London, 1596). Other editions were published in 1601 and 1614. Olivier the barber was granted the title and estates of the Comte de Meulan, not Dunois, in 1477 (*Philip de Comines*, 183, 247). Dunois was a different person, though of the same court and time.

131. There is no other record of this. Ralegh's first service seems to have been in France, where he fought with the Huguenots of Jarnac and Moncontour in 1569 (see *History of the World*, 5[2]:38). He went to Ireland as the captain of an infantry company in the summer of 1580 (Edward J. Thompson, *Sir Walter Ralegh* [London, 1935], 8, 17).

132. Arthur Grey, Baron Grey de Wilton (1536–93). He served as Lord Deputy of Ireland from July 1580 to August 1582. During this time he kept the Irish under control, but his methods were extreme and resulted in the slaughter of great numbers of the Irish.

133. Paraphrase of Horace, *Epistles*, 1. 1. 45:

> Impiger extremos curris mercator ad Indos,
> Per mare pauperiem fugiens, per saxa, per ignis.

> (Like an active merchant you rush to the farthest Indies,
> Fleeing poverty through sea, through rocks, through flames.)

134. From Cicero, *Paradoxa*, 1. 8: "Omnia mecum porto mea" (I carry all my belongings with me).

135. From Vergil, *Aeneid*, 1. 204:

> Per varios casus, per tot discrimina rerum
> Tendimus in Latium.

> (Through various mishaps, through so many perilous chances,
> We fare toward Latium.)

136. The difference occurred in the early part of 1582. Ralegh proposed that a greater concentration of effort be placed on winning over the smaller Irish chieftains rather than on a treaty with Desmond, and that the employment of the Irish Earl of Ormond by the English be discontinued. Grey's opinion of Ralegh's proposal was written to Lord Burghley:

> I doubt not but you will soon discern a difference between the judgments of those who, with grounded experience and approved reason, look into the condition of things, and those who, upon no ground but seeming fancies, and affecting credit with profit, frame "plots" upon impossibilities for others to execute. (Thompson, *Ralegh*, 24–25)

137. This famous "hanging tune" is mentioned by Shakespeare, Jonson, Nashe, and other writers of the period. The words (and music) are printed in William Chappell, *Popular Music of the Olden Times*, 2 vols. (London, 1859), 1:164:

> Fortune my foe why dost thou frown on me,
> And will thy favors never greater be?
> Wilt thou, I say, for ever breed me pain,
> And wilt thou not restore my joys again?

138. In the case of Ralegh, this passage is heavily ironic. Ralegh's reward from "her great successor" King James was to be imprisoned and executed, a fate in which Naunton played a part as a member of the King's Council. But as he does in other passages of the *Fragmenta*, Naunton is using Ralegh himself as a source. The passage referred to occurs in *History of the World*, 1(5):717–18:

> In my late sovereign's time, although for the wars which for her own safety she was constrained to undertake, Her Majesty had no less cause to use the service of martial men both by sea and land than any of her predecessors for many years had, yet, according to the destiny of that profession I do not remember that any of hers, the Lord Admiral excepted (her eldest and most prosperous commander), were either enriched or otherwise honored for any service by them performed. And that Her Majesty had many advised, valiant, and faithful men, the prosperity of her affairs did well witness, who in all her days never received dishonor by the cowardice or infidelity of any commander by herself chosen and employed.
>
> For as all her old captains by land died poor men . . . so those of a later and more dangerous employment, whereof Norris and Vere were the most famous, and who have done as great honor to our nation (for the means they had) as ever any did, those (I say) with many other brave colonels have left behind them (besides the reputation which they purchased with many travails and wounds) nor title nor estate to their posterity. As for the Lord Thomas Burrough and Peregrine Bertie, Lord Willoughby of Eresby, two very worthy and exceeding valiant commanders, they brought with them into the world their titles and estates. . . .
>
> But His Majesty hath already paid the greatest part of that debt. For besides the relieving by pensions all the poorer sort, he hath honored more martial men than all the kings of England have done for this hundred years.

139. Sir Fulke Greville, first Baron Brooke (1554–1628), was the author of the famous *Life of Sir Philip Sidney*, as well as other prose treatises, poetry, and plays. Except for "some fragments" none was published before 1633. He was educated at Shrewsbury (where he became intimate with Sidney) and went to Cambridge in 1568. He came to court with Sidney and became a favorite of the Queen. He was secretary for Wales from 1583 until his death; M.P. for Warwickshire, 1592–1620; treasurer of the wars and navy, 1598; Chancellor of the Exchequer, 1614–21; created peer, 1621. Naunton undoubtedly underestimates his ambition at court since Greville acquired considerable wealth in the last years of Elizabeth's reign and also under James.

140. Robert Devereux, second Earl of Essex (1566–1601); educated at Cambridge; created knight banneret for his bravery at Zutphen, 1586; became a favorite of Queen Elizabeth and Master of the Horse, 1587; K. G., 1588; married Frances, the widow of Sir Philip Sidney, thus displeasing Eizabeth, 1590; commanded a force sent to the help of Henry of Navarre, 1591; Privy Councillor, 1593; defeated the Spaniards in a naval battle off Cádiz, and took the town, 1596; Master of the Ordnance, 1597; set out on an expedition to the Azores, which proved a failure, 1597; Chancellor of Cambridge University, 1598; appointed Lieutenant and Governor-General of Ireland, 1599; forbidden to return to England and ordered to proceed to Ulster, 1599; made a truce, renewable every six weeks, with Tyrone, and returned to London in September 1599; accused before a specially constituted court of leaving his government and entering into a dishon-

orable and dangerous treaty with Tyrone, June 1600; set at liberty, August 1600; induced by others to contrive a plot for securing the dismissal of Elizabeth's councillors; attempted to raise the citizens of London, and was proclaimed a traitor, February 1601; tried and sentenced to death; executed, 25 February 1601.

141. In *A Parallel between Robert, Late Earl of Essex, and George, Late Duke of Buckingham* (London, 1641), 1: "The beginning of the Earl of Essex, I must attribute wholly or in great part to my Lord of Leicester: but yet as an introducer or supporter, not as a teacher: for as I go along, it will easily appear that he neither lived nor died by his discipline." Although this work was not printed until 1641, manuscript copies had been in circulation much earlier (Smith, *Wotton*, 1:206).

142. The titles of his father, Walter Devereux.

143. Naunton seems to accept the story of the poisoning of Devereux by Leicester.

144. Cf. Wotton, *Parallel between Essex and Buckingham*, 11:

But the first in eighty-eight at Tilbury Camp, was in my judgment, the very poison of all that followed. For there whilest the Queen stood in some doubt of a Spanish invasion (though it proved but a morris dance upon our waves) she made him in field Commander of the Cavalry (as he was before in court) and much graced him openly in view of the soldiers and people, even above my Lord of Leicester. The truth is from thenceforth he fed too fast.

145. "The beardless teaching the old." Thomas, Lord Borough, was sent in May 1597 as Lord Deputy of Ireland and commander of the army. Although Norris was not recalled, he was humiliated by the appointment of Borough, who was a personal antagonist during the Netherlands campaign. Norris died just a few months later.

146. which . . . him] G. b. 21; *omit* G. a. 11.

147. In *Parallel between Essex and Buckingham*, 12–13.

148. Thomas Sackville, first Earl of Dorset and Baron Buckhurst (1536–1608). In his early twenties he wrote the "Induction" and "The Complaint of Henry Duke of Buckingham" for *The Mirror for Magistrates*. In collaboration with Thomas Norton he wrote *Gorboduc*, the first English tragedy in blank verse. He was, however, primarily a statesman and occupied numerous offices at the court. Ultimately he was appointed Lord High Treasurer in 1599, a position he held until his death.

149. Naunton appears to be in error here. Sackville's father died in 1566, when Thomas was thirty years old and had already occupied positions of responsibility. There is no indication that his vast inheritance was encumbered in any way (see Arthur Collins, *The English Baronage* [London, 1727], 413).

150. From Ovid, *Ars Amatoria*, 1. 389: "Either do not attempt, or else persist."

151. Charles Blount, eighth Lord Mountjoy and Earl of Devonshire (1563–1606), came to the court about 1583. He was knighted in 1586, served in the Netherlands, the pursuit of the Armada, in Brittany, and in Essex's Azores expedition. He was appointed Lord Deputy of Ireland in 1601 and was successful in putting down Tyrone's rebellion. He was a lover of Penelope Rich, who was the wife of Lord Rich, sister of the Earl of Essex, and the model for the Stella of Sir Philip Sidney's sonnet sequence, "Astrophel and Stella." After Penelope's divorce from Lord Rich, she and Blount were married in December 1605.

152. James, the sixth Lord Mountjoy, lost much of the family estate as a result of business ventures in mining, and later spent large sums on alchemy. The older brother William's early death was said to have been brought on by debauchery (see C. B. Falls, *Mountjoy, Elizabethan General* [London, 1955], 19).

153. Robert Cecil, first Earl of Salisbury and first Viscount Cranbourne (1563–1612). He became a member of the Privy Council in 1591 and was appointed Secretary of State in 1596. He became Lord High Treasurer under King James in 1608.

154. Thomas Cecil (1542–1623) was created Earl of Exeter in 1605.

155. which] G. b. 20; and G. a. 11.

156. of weight] G. b. 21; *omit* G. a. 11.

157. that] G. b. 20; of G. a. 11.

158. out . . . had] G. b. 20; and out of a peculiar had G. a. 11.

159. I.e., sharp eyes.

160. I.e., Charles Blount, Lord Mountjoy.

161. without] G. b. 21; with G. a. 11.

162. Kinsale] Kingsale G. b. 21; Kingsade G. a. 11.

163. Cecil wrote a similar account of a rumored Spanish invasion of Ireland to George Carew on 29 August 1600; the letter to Devonshire probably belongs to the same time (see *Letters from Sir Robert Cecil to Sir George Carew*, ed. John Maclean [Westminster, 1864], 20).

164. The "scandal" of Salisbury's death (that he died in a roadside ditch of venereal disease) is repeated in Francis Osborne, *Traditional Memoirs on the Reign of King James* (London, 1658), 86–88. The final couplet indicates the general nature of the anonymous work:

> Till Atropos clapt him, a pox on the drab,
> For (spite of his tar box) he died of the scab.

165. Sir Francis Vere (1560–1609) served in the Netherlands from 1585 to 1604, except for taking part in the Cádiz expedition in 1596 and the Azores expedition in 1597. He was acting commander of the English troops in the service of the United Provinces of the Netherlands from 1589, and general from 1598.

166. From Ovid, *Metamorphoses*, 13. 140–41:

> Nam genus et proavos et quae non fecimus ipsi,
> vix ea nostro voco.

> (Our race and ancestry and the deeds that others have done,
> I call them in no true sense our own.)

167. for . . . camp] G. b. 21; *omit* G. a. 11.

168. in the . . . years] G. b. 20; *omit* G. a. 11.

169. Naunton's figures are inaccurate (see note 165, above).

170. Sir Horace Vere, Baron Vere of Tilbury (1565–1635).

171. Edward Somerset, fourth Earl of Worcester (1553–1628). He apparently did not hold any official position until 1590, when he was sent to Scotland to invest James VI with the Order of the Garter. He was appointed Deputy Master of the Horse in 1599 and was one of the peers selected to try Essex. In 1601 he was made Master of the Horse and became a member of the Privy Council.

172. I.e., Roman Catholicism.

Appendix. The Manuscript Copies

1.   Ronald B. McKerrow, *Prolegomena for the Oxford Shakespeare: A Study in Editorial Method* (Oxford, 1939), 36.

Bibliography

Academiae Cantabrigiensis Lachrymae. London, 1587.

"Arcana Aulica" . . . *To Which Is Added "Fragmenta Regalia."* London, 1694.

Bacon, Francis. *Collected Works.* Edited by J. Spedding, R. L. Ellis, and D. D. Heath. 14 vols. London, 1857–74.

————. *The Letters and the Life of Francis Bacon.* Edited by James Spedding. 7 vols. London, 1861–74.

Bertie, Georgina. *Five Generations of a Loyal House.* London, 1845.

Birch, Thomas. *Memoirs of the Reign of Queen Elizabeth.* 2 vols. London, 1754.

Black, John Bennett. *The Reign of Elizabeth, 1558–1603.* Oxford, 1936.

Bowyer, Robert. *The Parliamentary Diary of Robert Bowyer, 1606–1607.* Edited by D. H. Willson. Minneapolis, Minn., 1931.

Brooks, Eric St. John. *Sir Christopher Hatton.* London, 1946.

Cambridge University. *Alumni Cantabrigienses.* Edited by John Venn and J. A. Venn. 10 vols. Cambridge, 1922–54.

————. *The Book of Matriculations and Degrees . . . from 1544 to 1659.* Edited by John Venn and J. A. Venn. Cambridge, 1913.

Camden, William. *Annales Rerum Anglicarum et Hibernicarum Regnante Elizabetha.* London, 1615–27.

————. *The History of the Most Renowned and Victorious Princess Elizabeth, Late Queen of England.* Translated by R. Norton. London, 1630.

————. *The History of the Most Renowned and Victorious Princess Elizabeth, Late Queen of England.* 3d ed., rev. London, 1675.

[Caulfield, James.] *Memoirs of Sir Robert Naunton, Knt.* London, 1814. [Note: This work is a plagiarism of the section on Naunton in the third volume of Nichols' *The History and Antiquities of the County of Leicester.*]

Cecil, Robert. *Letters from Sir Robert Cecil to Sir George Carew.* Edited by John Mclean. Westminster, 1864.

Chamberlain, John. *The Letters of John Chamberlain.* Edited by Norman E. McClure. 2 vols. Philadelphia, 1939.

Chappell, William. *Popular Music of the Olden Times.* 2 vols. London, 1859.

Clapham, John. *Elizabeth of England: Certain Observations concerning the Life and Reign of Queen Elizabeth (1603).* Edited by Evelyn Plummer Read and Conyers Read. Philadelphia, 1951.

Coke, Dorothea. *The Last Elizabethan: Sir John Coke, 1563–1644.* London, 1937.

Collins, Arthur. *The English Baronage.* London, 1727.

————, ed. *Letters and Memorials of State . . . Written and Collected by Sir Henry Sidney . . . Sir Philip Sidney and His Brother Sir Robert Sidney. . . .* 2 vols. London, 1746.

Comines, Philippe de. *The History of Philip de Comines Knight, Lord of Argenton.* Translated by Thomas Danett. London, 1596.

Davies, Godfrey. *The Early Stuarts, 1603–1660.* Oxford, 1937.

Evans, Florence May. *The Principal Secretary of State: A Survey of the Office from 1558 to 1680.* Manchester, 1923.

Falls, C. B. *Mountjoy, Elizabethan General.* London, 1955.

The Fortesque Papers. Edited by S. R. Gardiner. Westminster, 1871.

Fuller, Thomas. *The History of the Worthies of England.* Edited by John Nichols. 2 vols. London, 1811.

Hadyn, Joseph. *The Book of Dignities.* London, 1890.

The Harleian Miscellany. 10 vols. London, 1808–13.

Harrison, George B. *A Second Elizabethan Journal.* New York, 1931.

Hentzner, P. *Paul Hentzner's Travels in England during the Reign of Queen Elizabeth.* Translated by Horace [Walpole], late Earl of Orford. London, 1797.

Herbert, Edward. *The Autobiography of Edward, Lord Herbert, of Cherbury.* Edited by Sidney L. Lee. London, 1886.

Howell, James. *Epistolae Ho-Elianae.* Edited by Joseph Jacobs. 2 vols. London, 1892.

Jermyn, James. *A Stemma of the Naunton Family.* British Library, Add. MS. 17098 (1806).

Jonson, Ben. *Conversations with William Drummond of Hawthornden.* Edited by R. F. Patterson. London, 1923.

Letters and Other Documents Illustrating the Relations between England and Germany at the Commencement of the Thirty Years' War. Edited by S. R. Gardiner. 2 vols. Westminster, 1865–68.

McKerrow, Ronald B. *A Dictionary of Printers and Booksellers in En-*

gland, Scotland and Ireland, and of Foreign Printers of English Books, 1557–1640. London, 1910.

———. "Edward Allde as a Typical Trade Printer," *Library*, 4th ser., 10 : 121–62.

———. *Prolegomena for the Oxford Shakespeare: A Study in Editorial Method.* Oxford, 1939.

Marañon, Gregorio. *Antonio Pérez.* Translated by Charles Ley. London, 1954.

Montague, F. C. *The History of England, 1603–1660.* London, 1907.

Naunton, Robert. *Fragmenta Regalia.* See Chapter 3 for the various editions of Naunton's work.

———. *Four Manuscripts concerning the Case of Robert Naunton vs. Robert Chester.* Huntington Library, MSS. EL-6055–EL-6058.

Nichols, John. *The History and Antiquities of the County of Leicester.* 4 vols. London, 1795–1815.

Osborne, Francis. *Traditional Memoirs on the Reign of King James.* London, 1658.

Peck, Francis, editor. *Desiderata Curiosa.* 2 vols. in 1. London, 1732–35.

Plomer, Henry R. *A Dictionary of the Booksellers and Printers Who Were at Work in England, Scotland, and Ireland from 1641 to 1667.* London, 1907.

———. "Eliot's Court Press, Decorative Blocks and Initials," *Library*, 4th ser., 3 : 194–209.

———. "The Eliot's Court Printing House, 1584–1674," *Library*, 4th ser., 2 : 175–84.

Ralegh, Sir Walter. *The History of the World.* London, 1614.

———. *The Prerogative of Parliaments in England.* Middelburg, 1628.

Read, Conyers. "Factions in the English Privy Council under Elizabeth," American Historical Association, *Annual Report for 1911,* 1 : 111–19.

———. *Mr. Secretary Cecil and Queen Elizabeth.* London, 1955.

———. *Mr. Secretary Walsingham and the Policy of Queen Elizabeth.* 3 vols. Oxford, 1925.

———. *The Tudors.* New York, 1936.

Rowse, Alfred L. *The England of Elizabeth.* New York, 1951.

Shaw, William A. *The Knights of England.* 2 vols. London, 1906.

Smith, D. Nichol. *Characters from the Histories and Memoirs of the Seventeenth Century.* Oxford, 1918.

Smith, Logan Pearsall. *The Life and Letters of Sir Henry Wotton.* 2 vols. Oxford, 1907.

Thompson, Edward J. *Sir Walter Ralegh.* London, 1935.

United Kingdom. Historical Manuscripts Commission. Reports. London, 1870–1957.

———. *Members of Parliament.* 4 vols. London, 1878–91.

———. *Calendar of State Papers, Domestic Series . . . 1547–1625.* 12 vols. London, 1856–72.

———. *Calendar of State Papers relating to Scotland, 1547–1603.* 13 vols. Edinburgh and Glasgow, 1898–1969.

———. *Calendar of State Papers and Manuscripts relating to English Affairs, Existing in the Archives and Collections of Venice, and in Other Libraries of Northern Italy.* 38 vols. London, 1864–1947.

Wentworth, Thomas, first Earl of Strafford. *The Earl of Strafford's Letters and Dispatches.* Edited by William Knowler. 2 vols. Dublin, 1740.

Whitelocke, James. *Liber Famelicus.* Edited by John Bruce. Westminster, 1858.

Willson, D. Harris. *King James VI and I.* London, 1956.

Wilson, Arthur. *The History of Great Britain, Being the Life and Reign of King James the First.* London, 1653.

Wilson, Mona. *Sir Philip Sidney.* London, 1931.

Wotton, Henry. *A Parallel between Robert, Late Earl of Essex, and George, Late Duke of Buckingham.* London, 1641.

———. *The State of Christendom; or, A Most Exact and Curious Discovery of Many Secret Passages, and Hidden Mysteries of the Times.* London, 1657.

Name Index to the *Fragmenta Regalia*